DISSECTING ADL'S 2015 FARRAKHAN: IN HIS OWN WORDS

VOLUME 1

2021

BY GABRIEL LOPEZ

**Dissecting ADL's 2015
Farrakhan: In His Own Words**

Copyright 2021 Gabriel Lopez

This book is dedicated to the Honorable Minister and Messiah Louis Farrakhan, student of the living Christ, the Most Honorable Elijah Muhammad and to all who stand on the Truth taught by these two servants of Allah (God), Who came in the person of Master Fard Muhammad, and to all believers in the oneness of Allah (God), no matter which religion or faith they practice.

To my lovely fiancée, Paula, for me not having been completely present for you during the redaction of this book. Praises be to Allah for your patience and understanding of the importance of this work for me. Hopefully, He will remove some of my sins.

Email: DissectingTexts@gmail.com
Facebook: @GabrielLopezTextDissector
Special thanks:
Proofreading by: https://akaenu.com/
Cover & Formatting By: Anointed Hands Digital Marketing | Neosalamana | Rakib
The Nation of Islam

Master Fard Muhammad   The Honorable Elijah Muhammad

The Honorable Louis Farrakhan

Images from Google

Table of content

Introduction

Report analyzed: *Farrakhan: In His Own Words*[1]
Written by the Anti-Defamation League (ADL)
Published 2014 and updated: March 20, 2015

In the name of Allah, The Beneficent, The Merciful, Who came in the person of Master Fard Muhammad,

This analysis will demonstrate who is telling the truth and who is distorting it or lying. Do notice that the ADL has been putting much pressure on many platforms to censor the Nation of Islam and the Teachings of the Most Honorable Elijah Muhammad through the Honorable Minister Louis Farrakhan Muhammad. So, many videos are not available anymore and need to be purchased on the Final Call Store[2].

To reduce the number of words in this text, the Most Honorable (and Christ) Elijah Muhammad will be referred as "Elijah Muhammad" and the Honorable Minister (and Messiah) Louis Farrakhan Muhammad will be referred as "Farrakhan". There is no intention to disrespect or to minimize the importance of these servants of Allah by doing so.

This analysis is made possible thanks to the many books, articles and lectures I have been able to read and watch; a lot of which come from the Nation of Islam. However, this analysis should <u>not</u> be considered biased because of it. I make sure to try to present to the reader the sources from which the NOI research team and scholars use and provide to prove their point. So, the praises go to Allah through the people who have researched the many issues we are about to touch. Sure, I have done my part of research to hopefully bring more to the table, but this work is inspired by the work done by others, whether from the NOI or not, in the purpose of advancing the

---

[1] ADL, *Farrakhan in his own words*, 2013, pp. 1-2:
https://www.adl.org/sites/default/files/documents/assets/pdf/anti-semitism/united-states/farrakhan-in-his-own-words-2015-03-20.pdf.

[2] The Final Call Store online: https://store.finalcall.com/.

truth. I just gathered the information and will present it to you in my own writing style which I hope you will enjoy. By the help of Allah, it will be clear enough for you to understand each argument and consequently, getting as close as possible to the absolute Truth which is known by Allah and His Christ.

When the ADL doesn't make a direct quote **and** doesn't provide a link or enough information to find the source where we can all hear with our own ears what they claim and get the full context in which the alleged words were said, the reader is invited to be very cautious to accept the ADL's claims at face value. This type of situation is quite frequent and becomes evident very early in their report. Some of those claims I will touch on if I feel comfortable enough with it to destroy a blatant lie, even if it is not related to something allegedly said by Farrakhan.

As you will be able to realize in this analysis, even when Farrakhan is rightfully quoted, his detractors and enemies inject their own distorted interpretation which denatures what he has said. Therefore, it becomes a lie put on him.

The Holy Qur'an Maulana Muhammad Ali's translation is the one used in this book for quotes.

Holy Qur'an chapter 49, verse 6:

> *O you who believe, **if an unrighteous man brings you news, look carefully into it, lest you harm a people in ignorance**, then be sorry for what you did.*

Image from Amazon

You will also notice that the ADL treats the Jewish people as an indivisible whole. This goes against what God Himself warns the Believers of. Indeed, there are two types of Jews (or Christians, Muslims, etc.). Either one is a Jew inwardly; meaning one who has integrated the principles of the Torah in his spirit and mind and tries to live the life of a Righteous servant of God; or one is a Jew outwardly; meaning one who claims to be a Jew but cannot back it up in works and deeds. The Bible says it better in the book of Romans.

The King James Version is the one used in this book for quotes.

Romans chapter 2, verses 28 and 29:

28 For he is not a Jew, which is one outwardly; neither is that circumcision, which is outward in the flesh:

29 But he is a Jew, which is one inwardly; and circumcision is that of the heart, in the spirit, and not in the letter; whose praise is no of men, but of God.

Image from Kobo

Revelation chapter 2 and 3, verse 9 for both chapters:

> *9 I know thy works, and tribulation, and poverty, (but thou art rich) and I know **the blasphemy of them which say they are Jews, and are not, but are the Synagogue of Satan.***

> *9 Behold, **I will make them of the Synagogue of Satan, which say they are Jews, and are not, but do lie**; behold, I will make them to come and worship before thy feet, and to know that I have loved thee.*

The Holy Qur'an also points out those so-called Jews (Satanic) who alter the words and disobey willingly the One God.

Chapter 4, verse 46:

> **Some of those who are Jews alter words from their places and say, we have heard, and we disobey**; *and (say), Hear without being made to hear, and (say), Ra'i-na, **distorting with their tongues and slandering religion**. And if they had said, We hear and we obey, and hearken, and unzur-na, it would have been*

*better for them and more upright; but Allah has cursed them on account of their disbelief, **so they believe not but a little***.

That part "so they believe not but a little" indicates that most of those who call themselves "Jews" are not truly Jews but rather posers. Just like the outward Jew mentioned before; claiming to be something he is not. It is once again highlighted in chapter 5, verse 66:

> **And if they had observed the Torah** *and the Gospel and that which is revealed to them from their Lord, they would certainly have eaten from above them and from beneath their feet.* **There is a party of them keeping to the moderate course**; *and most of them — evil is that which they do*.

Allah certainly knows what is in the heart of them who He gives life to. So, the little party of them who believe and who can claim the name "Jew" are those who keep the Torah as guidance. So, what are the majority of those who claim to be Jews follow? Verse 79 of chapter 2 in the Holy Qur'an gives us the answer.

> *Woe!* **then to those who write the Book with their hands then say, this is from Allah**; *so that they may take for it a small price.* **So, woe! to them for what their hands write** *and woe! to them for what they earn.*

This is clearly a reference to the Talmud. It is important to emphasize that **the Talmud is not Judaism**.

The Torah <u>is</u> the basis of Judaism.

What do the modern Jew follows? Well, according to the late Michael Levi Rodkinson who is known for being the first to have translated the <u>Babylonian Talmud to English</u>[3]:

> **The modern Jew is the product of the Talmud**…

---

[3] Michael L. Rodkinson, *The Babylonian Talmud*, Volumes 1-10, (1918), pp 3225: <u>https://www.jewishvirtuallibrary.org/jsource/Judaism/FullTalmud.pdf</u>.

Shouldn't the modern Jew be the product of the Law of God (Torah)?

Michael Levi Rodkinson (1845-1904)

Image from Wikipedia

For those who follow the Torah, the Holy Qur'an mentions them in a favorable manner.

Chapter 2 verse 62:
*Surely those who believe, **and those who are Jews**, and the Christians, and the Sabians, **whoever believes in Allah and the Last Day and does good, they have their reward with their Lord**, and there is no fear for them, nor shall they grieve.*

Chapter 5 verse 69:
*Surely those who believe and **those who are Jews** and the Sabians and the Christians — **whoever believes in Allah and the Last Day and does good** — they shall have no fear nor shall they grieve.*

And before starting the analysis, let us get the so-called "anti-Semite" argument out of the way.

<u>First, who is a Semite?</u>

The Merriam-Webster online dictionary <u>states</u>[4]:

> 1. *a: a member of any of a number of peoples of ancient southwestern Asia including the Akkadians, Phoenicians, Hebrews, and Arabs.*

The first known use of the word 'Semite' defined as above is from 1598 according to the online dictionary. Another definition given from the same source states:

> *A member of a group of people originally of southwestern Asia that includes Jews and Arabs.*

The Jewish Virtual Library <u>states</u>[5] :

> *The term Semite is linguistically related to the name Shem",* who is a son of Noah.

The prefix "anti" means against. So, to be an anti-Semite means to be against the group of people mentioned previously. This means against Jews, Arabs, Phoenicians, Hebrews, etc.

But who gave birth to those groups, if it is not the original men and women of the Earth? So consequently, Black people being the Original people of the Earth and possessing in their genes the power to produce all races, Black people could also be considered Semitic. But that would diminish the fact that they are universal and direct descendants of Allah (God) as He created them in His image and likeness.

<u>Second, is Farrakhan an anti-Semite?</u>

His enemies, who claim to be Jews, say so because he is critical of them. But, by definition, as seen previously, he cannot be one.

---

[4] From the Merriam-Webster online dictionary: https://www.merriam-webster.com/dictionary/Semites.

[5] *Shem*, Jewish Virtual Library: https://www.jewishvirtuallibrary.org/shem.

Furthermore, how could he be accused of being pro-Arab and anti-Semite at the same time since Arabs are also Semites as he mentioned in a 1984 interview with Mme Sandi Freeman? Please watch the interview[6] starting at 20 minutes 26 seconds.

Image from YouTube

His enemies could easily say that the previous argument is playing with semantics. **The Anti-Defamation League** actually does that[7]:

> *Quite simply, anti-Semitism refers to the hatred of Jews, <u>whatever the nationality, race, color or creed of the perpetrator</u>. Attempting to dismiss the term anti-Semitism because of semantics does not erase the fact of its existence or its history.*

So, the ADL claims ownership of the term "anti-Semitism" or "anti-Semitic". Who gave them the right to do that? And notice that their definition of anti-Semitism implies that even Jews could be labeled anti-Semites. In front of such contradictions, we can only conclude that the ADL's definition is deceiving and wrong at best. Besides, Ashkenazi Jews are not even Semites unlike the Sephardic Jews.

So, people like Mr. Alan Dershowitz, Mr. Jonathan Greenblatt and Mr. Abraham Foxman are not even Semitic! And when Israeli police officers mistreat the ultra-orthodox Jews in the streets, such as in

---

[6] Minister Farrakhan with Sandi Freeman on the *Freeman Report*, June 28, 1984: https://www.youtube.com/watch?v=kJOPkx9eozY.

[7] The online page access has been restricted to the public (August 2021): https://www.adl.org/resources/fact-sheets/response-to-common-inaccuracy-arabs-cannot-be-anti-semitic.

these videos here[8] or here[9], does it qualify them as anti-Semites? When the Israeli army killed Arabs in Lebanon or in the ongoing genocide in Gaza, doesn't that make them anti-Semites?

I want you to take a good look to real anti-Jewish sentiment by New York City Councilman David Greenfield[10]:

*In a confrontation at a New York City Council Meeting in 2016, Councilman **David Greenfield told Neturei Karta leader Rabbi Yisroel David Weiss** that **"you represent two dozen mentally unstable individuals, that's all, and you are the leader of this mentally unstable cult"***

NYC Councilman David Greenfield

Image from Wikipedia

And the article dares to claim Reps. Ocasio-Cortez, Omar and Rashida Tlaib brought anti-Semitism with the presence of the Neturei Karta rabbis.

---

[8] The Associated Press, *Hundreds of ultra-Orthodox Jews clash with Israeli police*, March 12, 2018. The video shows a protest by Ultra-Orthodox Jews and being roughed up by the Israeli police: https://www.youtube.com/watch?v=JFIcaGpg8IU.

[9] The Associated Press, *Israeli police arrest 8 in ultra-Orthodox military protest*, September 17, 2018. The video shows Ultra-Orthodox Jews being violently removed from the streets or arrested by Israeli police: https://www.youtube.com/watch?v=tm1F8rs7oMc&t.

[10] Coalition for Jewish Values, *Rabbis Thank Neturei Karta for "Unmistakable Proof" of Anti-Semitism in Congress*, March 11, 2019: https://coalitionforjewishvalues.org/2019/03/rabbis-thank-neturei-karta-for-unmistakable-proof-of-anti-semitism-in-congress/.

Neturei Karta Rabbis

Image from nkusa.org

And what about this horrendous quote from the first Interior Minister of the State of Israel, so-called Jew Yitzhak Gruenbaum:

One cow in Palestine is worth more than all the Jews in Europe.[11]

So, is Farrakhan an anti-Semite? The answer is no. On top of his 87 years of age, there is yet to be found a single act of anti-Semitism (or anti-Jew) by him. He has mentioned in many lectures that he respects the Jewish community.

Listen to what he said to Mme Freeman starting at 37 minutes 10 seconds of the interview mentioned previously:

S.F.: Perhaps we can get a very clear understanding this evening as far as your feelings toward the Jews.

*L.F.M.: Let me say this very humbly. You know, **I have no hatred or animosity toward Jews**. (...) **I'm not hateful of Jews. I have great respect for Jews**.*

After being banned from Facebook in 2019, Farrakhan was invited by Father Michael Pfleger to St. Sabina Church where he reiterated

---

[11] Torah Jews, *Yom HaShoah In "Israel" - The Art Of Fabrication*. The word "Europe" is sometimes replaced by "Poland" depending on the source. Here, it mentions Europe: https://www.tructorahjews.org/yom-hashoah-%E2%80%9Cisrael%E2%80%9D-art-fabrication.

that he is not a hater of the Jews. Starting at 1 hour 26 minutes and 49 seconds, he says[12]:

*I have not said one word of hate. **I do not hate Jewish people**. Not one that is with me has ever committed a crime against the Jewish people; Black people; White people; no matter what your color is. As long as you don't attack us, we don't bother you.*

But he <u>has come</u> to separate the good Jews (followers of the Torah) of the Satanic Jews (followers of the Talmud). Start the previous video at St. Sabina at 1 hour 25 minutes 17 seconds.

Father Michael Pfleger with Farrakhan at St. Sabina Church

Image from the Final Call Newspaper online

Furthermore, in his July 4th 2020 message to the world, The Criterion[13], he gives honor to the name "Jews" by saying to his enemies usurping that good name that… just listen for yourselves starting at 1 hour 40 minutes and 57 seconds:

---

[12] The Faith Community of Saint Sabina, *Minister Farrakhan - Response to Facebook*, Thursday, May 9, 2019 at the Faith Community of Saint Sabina: https://www.youtube.com/watch?v=3nvaUB1qIfE. If not available on YouTube: https://finalcallstore.noi.org/product/wearefarrakhan-community-rally/.

[13] Minister Louis Farrakhan, *The Criterion*, July 4, 2020: https://www.noi.org/the-criterion/ or https://finalcallstore.noi.org/product/the-criterion/.

> *Those of you that say that you are Jews… **I will not even give you the HONOR** of calling you a Jew. **You are not a Jew. You're a so-called (Jew).** You're Satan.*

And if Farrakhan is what his enemies claim, how do they explain the gift (silver chalice and plate) given to him by two rabbis on which it is written and can be seen on twitter[14]:

> *To the honorable Minister Louis Farrakhan*
> ***You are the Messiah of the World***
> *and to every human who wants to be civilized*
> *Your friend and admirer*
> ***Rabbi Shlomo Mordecia Hager***

Please watch[15] his keynote address at Saviours' Day 2019 starting at 4 hours 23 minutes and 28 seconds in which he presents the gift he received (and many others).

Silver plate given to Farrakhan

Image from Abdul Qiyam Muhammad's twitter account

---

[14] Tweet by Brother Abdul Qiyam Muhammad, February 17, 2019.

[15] Minister Louis Farrakhan, *A Saviour Is Born For the Whole of Humanity: No One Need Perish*, February 17, 2019, Saviours' Day. The video from YouTube has been censored, so one needs to buy the DVD (or CD) here: https://finalcallstore.noi.org/product/saviours-day-2019-keynote-address/.

So, we can conclude that Farrakhan is neither an anti-Semite nor an Anti-Jew.

Can we say as much about the Ashkenazi (so-called) Jews like Ariel Sharon, Vladimir Zhabotinsky, Avraham Stern or former Minister of Justice Ayelet Shaked who wished "death on all Palestinians while supporting the Israeli military assault[16]"

Ayelet Shaked, former Minister of Justice of Israel

Image from Wikipedia

Or what about the Israeli government that injects birth control on Ethiopian immigrants[17]?

So, using the term "anti-Semite" or "anti-Semitism" is quite frivolous and unproductive. It only serves to deflect a discussion, most of the time, rather than to define a person.

This was just the introduction of the book. So, get excited!

---

[16] Daily Sabah, *'Mothers of all Palestinians should also be killed,' says Israeli politician*, July 14, 2014: https://www.dailysabah.com/mideast/2014/07/14/mothers-of-all-palestinians-should-also-be-killed-says-israeli-politician.

[17] Elise Knutsen, *Israel Forcibly Injected African Immigrants with Birth Control, Report Claims*, January 28, 2013, Forbes. Ethiopian Jewish women being mandatorily injected with contraceptives: https://www.forbes.com/sites/eliseknutsen/2013/01/28/israel-foribly-injected-african-immigrant-women-with-birth-control/#26709a2767b8.

Chapter 1:
First page, first sentence, first deception

The report has a header that mentions "Imagine a World without hate". This is ludicrous because Allah (God) hates evil. Here are some examples from the Bible (King James Version).

Proverb 6: 16 to 19

> *16 **These six things doth the Lord hate**: yea, seven are an abomination unto him:*
> *17 A proud look, a lying tongue, and hands that shed innocent blood,*
> *18 A heart that deviseth wicked imaginations, feet that be swift in running to mischief,*
> *19 A false witness that speaketh lies, and he that soweth discord among brethren.*

Proverb 8: 13

> ***The fear of the Lord is to hate evil**: pride, and arrogancy, and the evil way, and the froward mouth, do I hate.*

Isaiah 61: 8

> ***For I the Lord** love judgment, I **hate robbery for burnt offering**; and I will direct their work in truth, and I will make an everlasting covenant with them.*

So, hating evil is natural and normal. Why would a world be without hate of injustice?

The deception is on…

Chapter 2:
The report's introductive claims

Section 1 - Page 1, paragraph 1 of the ADL's report

Farrakhan has marked himself as a notable figure on the extremist scene verbally attacking Jews…

The ADL starts its report with three claims on the first paragraph.

> *For over 30 years, Louis Farrakhan, leader of the Nation of Islam (NOI),* **has marked himself** *as* **a notable figure on the extremist scene**, **verbally attacking** *Jews, white people and the LGBT community.*

The first claim is that he "marked himself". In reality, the <u>Synagogue of Satan</u> has marked him as whatever claims it makes about him.

The claim about extremism can be explained by the contrary nature of the people embodying the ADL. When you have people that scheme and lie about others since 1913, and then people stand up to their lies, they call it extremism. As Farrakhan has taught from the teachings of the Most Honorable Elijah Muhammad: we are in a time when Allah is present. Evidently, the God of this falling world, Satan, will highly oppose those who represent righteousness. Hence, Farrakhan is categorized as an extremist by wicked (or ignorant) people.

As for the claim about "verbally attacking", it is worthy of mention that they implicitly admit that Farrakhan never physically attacked anyone. Now, you will notice that the enemy of Truth will skillfully use words to try to provoke an emotional reaction instead of triggering an analytical mindset.

Here we have a blatant example by the ADL on how to deceptively lead the reader toward its goal: to break the magnetism of Farrakhan.

Instead of what they claim to be "attacking (Jews)," Farrakhan is simply critical about different issues.

The ADL even decided to single out three groups they consider 'attacked' by Farrakhan: Jews, White people and the LGBTQ. It provides in its report at the middle of the second page many quotes by him, which will be analyzed and given context to in further volumes, Allah willing.

In recent years, he embarked on a wide-ranging campaign featuring some of the most hateful speeches of his career as head of the NOI

The ADL claims that:

> **In recent years**, *Farrakhan has embarked on a wide-ranging campaign specifically targeting the Jewish community, which has featured* **some of the most hateful speeches** *of* **Farrakhan's career** *as* <u>head of the NOI</u>.

There are many problems in that sentence. For starters, Minister Farrakhan joined the Nation of Islam in 1955 under <u>the eternal leadership of Elijah Muhammad</u>. After the complete dismantling of the NOI that started in 1975 by a son of Elijah Muhammad, Farrakhan started its rebuilding around 1977. Contrary to the claim that it is "in recent years" that Farrakhan "embarked on a wide-ranging campaign" (of resurrection I would suggest), the controversy with Jews started decades ago and precisely in 1983 during the presidential campaign of Reverend Jesse Jackson. How it began is explained in this July 21, 2020 article[18] (The Controversy with the Jews: What is the Truth?) by the Nation of Islam Research Group. The article makes it clear that members of the Jewish community targeted Farrakhan for daring to defend his brother (Jesse Jackson) from their attacks against his presidential campaign such as this advertisement[19] in November 11, 1983 New York Times. After a lecture on February 23, 1984, defending Rev. Jesse Jackson, Minister Farrakhan was labeled as a "Black Hitler" on February 27, 1984, and it has never stopped from there.

---

[18] Nation of Islam Research Group, *The Controversy with the Jews: What is the Truth?*, July 21, 2020: https://new.finalcall.com/2020/07/21/the-controversy-with-the-jews-what-is-the-truth/.

[19] Scan of "Jews Against Jackson" New York Times ad of November 11, 1983: https://5j6.062.myftpupload.com/wp-content/uploads/2012/03/RuinJesseRuin.NYT_.11.11.1983.p.A24.png.

DO YOU BELIEVE THAT ANY JEW SHOULD SUPPORT THIS MAN?

SHOULD *ANY* DECENT AMERICAN?

WE BELIEVE THAT JESSE JACKSON IS A DANGER TO AMERICAN JEWS. TO THE STATE OF ISRAEL AND TO AMERICA ITSELF. AND WE ARE APPALLED AT THE ABSOLUTE SILENCE OF THE LIBERAL COMMUNITY AND, MOST IMPORTANTLY, OF JEWISH LEADERS AND ORGANIZATIONS!

Article by the New York Times attacking Rev. Jesse Jackson

Image 1 of 3

Consider this:

- "When it came to the division of power we did not get from the Jews the slice of cake we deserved... the Jews do not share with us control of wealth, broadcasting stations and other centers of power."

(Jesse Jackson on CBS' Sixty Minutes, Sep. 16, 1979)

- "The conflict (with the Jews) began when we started our quest for power. Jews were willing to share decency but not power."

(Jesse Jackson in The N.Y. Times, Aug. 19, 1979)

- "One who does not think (Yasir) Arafat is a true hero does not read the situation correctly."

(Jesse Jackson in Israel, as quoted in Israel's largest newspaper, Maariv, September 27, 1979)

- "Arafat is educated, urbane, reasonable. I think his commitment to justice is an absolute one." (Jesse Jackson in Penthouse magazine, Feb. 1981)

- "Jesse Jackson blames Israel for tying the hands of the U.S. and endangering her national and economic interests... He warned against a development of anti-Semitism if Israel continued to erode American interests." (Maariv, September 25, 1979)

In light of these outrageous statements against Jews and Israel, and in view of Jackson's support of the PLO architects of murder of women and children, we ask?

HOW CAN JEWISH LEADERSHIP BE SO UTTERLY SILENT? HAD JESSE JACKSON BEEN WHITE, WOULD THE LIBERAL ESTABLISHMENT AND JEWISH LEADERSHIP BE SO CRAVENLY TIMID?

We believe that Jesse Jackson is far more powerful then most think. We believe that he is successfully building a coalition of malcontents who will be a disaster for Jews, for Israel, for America, for the free world. We believe that he is successfully moving to a position of power within the Democratic party. *We are afraid and we intend to act.*

WE ARE FORMING CHAPTERS OF *JEWS AGAINST JACKSON* in every community for the purpose of alerting Jews and non Jews, alike, to the very real threat this man represents. We intend to pressure national and local political leaders to openly condemn Jesse Jackson and cut all political ties and funds to him. WE WILL EXPOSE JESSE JACKSON FOR THE DANGER HE REALLY IS: *RUIN, JESSE, RUIN.*

As Jews and as Americans you have a deep obligation to join us and DO. The Jackson machine is more powerful than you know and we must stop it. YOU *CAN* STOP IT.

TODAY, fill out the coupon below and help us with the desperately needed funds to make this a nationwide campaign of success. BECOME INVOLVED. Help set up a local Jews Against Jackson group in your neighborhood NOW.

Article by the New York Times attacking Rev. Jesse Jackson

Image 2 of 3

JESSE JACKSON IS NO GOOD FOR JEWS, FOR ISRAEL OR FOR
AMERICA. STOP HIM. *RUIN JESSE, NOW.*

I, too, am afraid of Jesse Jackson's threat and want to join in stopping him.

_______________ Enclosed is my contribution of $ _______________

_______________ I want to start a local chapter of Jews Against Jackson in my community. Please contact me.

NAME _______________________________ PHONE_____________

ADDRESS ____

Please make checks payable to: Jews Against Jackson and mail to:
1316 Kings Highway, Brooklyn, N.Y. 11229. Attn: Fern Rosenblatt-Director

Article by the New York Times attacking Rev. Jesse Jackson

Image 3 of 3

They called for: Ruin Jesse, Ruin.

Then, we must consider that the terms "hateful speeches" is just another trick by deceptive people. This is simply because, as stated already, one either speaks the truth or falsehood. Each can provoke an emotional reaction that can be either hatred, passion, joy, etc. What is most important here is to figure out who is telling the truth and who is lying. I assert that Farrakhan tells the truth and that his opposition purposely lies about him.

Lastly about that brief quote from the ADL's report, one has to keep in mind that Elijah Muhammad is the head of the Nation of Islam. This can be confirmed by Farrakhan who repeats over and over at the beginning of many of his lectures/messages (if not all of them) that he is a student of Elijah Muhammad (the teacher). He has also mentioned that he has been put on his (Elijah Muhammad's) seat in his (Elijah Muhammad's) absence. He is the extension of Elijah Muhammad; the same as Aaron was to Moses.

In *Closing the Gap* by Jabril Muhammad, page 365, Farrakhan explains when Elijah Muhammad verbally whipped him in front of others while at the same time informing all of them that he was second to him alone.

He's whipping me in the presence of all of those who dislike me. **But he's telling them at the same time, in the Nation I'm second only to him**. *So, he's lifting me and beating me and teaching me and trying me because now I'm a big man in the nation, see.*[20]

Now, since Saviours' Day 1981, he has been telling the whole world that Elijah Muhammad is physically alive and on the Wheel designed by Master Fard Muhammad, Allah in the flesh.

At Saviours' Day 2018, he thanks Allah for Elijah Muhammad. Listen to his words starting at 59 minutes 48 seconds of this video[21]:

I thank Him (Master Fard Muhammad) for **my teacher**. *I thank Him for* **my leader**. *I thank Him for* **my guide**. *I thank him (Elijah Muhammad) for being the father I never had. I thank Him for allowing me to stay* **the course** *for 62 years and 4 months* **in the classroom of God**.

This is consistent with Scriptures. See John 5: 30 (KJV):

I can of mine own self do nothing: *as I hear, I judge: and my judgment is just; because I seek not mine own will, but* **the will of the Father which hath sent me**.

Jewish people were responsible of the slave trade

The ADL claims that:

Farrakhan has alleged that the **Jewish people were responsible for the slave trade**...

Here is an example of a claim that does not provide a direct quote or a link to a speech or lecture by Farrakhan. So, this should be considered a straw man fallacy. We can assume so because if Farrakhan would have said so, the ADL would have just cited where,

---

[20] Jabril Muhammad, *Closing the Gap*, Chicago, Il: FNC Publishing Co., 2006, p. 365.

[21] Minister Louis Farrakhan, *Saviours' Day 2018 Keynote Address*, February 25, 2018: https://www.youtube.com/watch?v=WDd7QVm151U or here if deleted: https://finalcallstore.noi.org/product/saviours-day-2018-keynote-address/.

when and in what occasion it would have been said. We are just left to accept at face value their claim that he said so, which we will not of course.

Well, it is a matter of historical and undeniable facts, which can be found in both books by the Historical Research Department of the Nation of Islam, *The Secret Relationship Between Blacks and Jews*, gathered by Jewish scholars, such as Dr. Harold Brackman, and scholars that are not considered anti-Semitic, of the prominent involvement[22] of so-called Jews in those activities. As seen in the link provided and made available by the Nation of Islam, Dr. Brackman's 1977 dissertation stated that:

> ***There is no denying*** *that the Babylonian Talmud was the first source to read a **Negrophobic content** into the episode by stressing Canaan's fraternal connection with Cush.*

> *During the 1600's, in fact, **slave trading in Brazil became a 'Jewish' mercantile speciality in much the same way it had been in early medieval Europe.***

The reader is invited to read all the dissertation's excerpts provided by the Nation of Islam.

I will point out the following arguments, although the books by the Historical Research Department of the Nation of Islam have already built the unbreakable case of Jewish involvement in the oppression of Black people during slavery and after the so-called liberation. The following arguments were made possible thanks to their books.

---

[22] Nation of Islam Research Group, *CONFESSIONS OF A JEWISH RACIST: DR. HAROLD BRACKMAN*, August 11, 2016: https://noirg.org/articles/confessions-of-a-jewish-racist-dr-harold-brackman/.

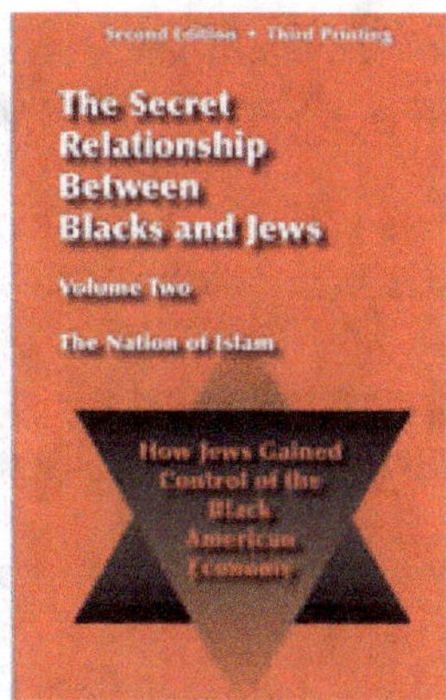

The Secret Relationship Between Blacks & Jews, Volume 1 and 2

Image from the Final Call Newspaper's article by Abdul Arif Muhammad[23]

In the Talmud[24] (Volume 1, chapter 2, page 41) it is written that to be considered rich one has to:

*The rabbis taught: **"Who may consider himself rich***?*" One who enjoys his riches, is the opinion of R. Meir. R. Tarphon says: **He who has** a hundred fields, a hundred vineyards, **and a hundred slaves at work in them**. R. Aqiba said: He who has a wife adorned with good virtues. R. Jose said: He who has a place for man's necessity in his house.*

Where does the Hamitic curse come from which makes Black people the cursed ones? It is from the Babylonian Talmud Sanhedrin chapter 11 section 108b[25], by Ph. D Harry Freedman under the editorship of Rabbi Dr I. Epstein:

Our Rabbis taught: Three copulated in the ark, and they were all punished — the dog, the raven, and Ham. The dog was doomed to

---

[23] Abdul Arif Muhammad, *A Response to Alan Dershowitz, Esq. 'YOU ARE OF YOUR FATHER THE DEVIL (SATAN)'*, The Final Call Digital Newspapers, July 9, 2020: https://www.mydigitalpublication.com/publication/?i=667008&article_id=3718791&view=articleBrowser.

[24] See footnote 3.

[25] Source: English translation of the Talmud, chapter 11, by Rabbi Harry Freedman, available online on Halakhah.com: http://halakhah.com/sanhedrin/sanhedrin_108.html.

be tied; the raven expectorates [his seed into his mate's mouth]. **and Ham was smitten in his skin.**[34]

The footnote 34 tells us: "I.e., **from him descended Cush (the negro) who is black-skinned.**"

To further demonstrate that it is in (satanic) Jewish roots to regard Blacks as inferiors, meet late Louisiana congressman William M. (Mallory) Levy[26], a former Confederate Army military and a Democrat congressman of Louisiana.

In 1877, he sold to the Congress the infamous Wormley Hotel deal. This deal was to put Rutherford B. Hayes as President of the USA in exchange that the South would not suffer the presence of the Federal authority or Army in its way it treated slaves. His full speech can be found here[27] on pages 2046 and 2047. Can you imagine a Democrat elevating a Republican to Presidency? Well, yes if there is a gain in doing such.

> *The people of Louisiana have solemn, earnest, and, I believe, truthful assurances from prominent members of the Republican party,* **high in the confidence of Mr. Hayes, that in the event of his elevation to the Presidency he will be guided by a policy of conciliation toward the Southern States,** *that he will not use the Federal authority or the Army to force upon those States governments not of their choice, but in the case of these States will leave their own people to settle the matter peaceably, of themselves.*

Of course, he claimed that the atrocities against the Black people in his State by white people were just a misrepresentation:

> *I know that the people of Louisiana,* **the white people of Louisiana, have been most cruelly and grossly misrepresented,** *I*

---

[26] Source: Biographical Directory of the United States Congress, as reported on the Jewish Virtual Library: https://www.jewishvirtuallibrary.org/william-mallory-levy.

[27] Congressional record—House, March 1, 1977, pp. 2046-2047: https://www.govinfo.gov/content/pkg/GPO-CRECB-1877-pt3-v5/pdf/GPO-CRECB-1877-pt3-v5-9-2.pdf.

*know that for party purposes and for selfish ends **there have been
ascribed to them the most shocking barbarities and the violation
of every rule of civilization and enlightenment**. These slanders
have been most industriously circulated and have served to excite
prejudice and sectional animosity against us*

Therefore, he dismissed the crimes against Black people done in
Louisiana as slanderous. Are: the Colfax, the Coushatta, Opelousas
massacres by the White League slanderous claims or facts?

And then he claimed that white people of Louisiana would treat
fairly all citizens:

*I know, and I pledge my word and my honor to the truth of the
declaration, (...) that the white people of Louisiana, (...) will in
the administration of the government of the State, in its executive,
legislative, and judicial departments, **extend equal and impartial
justice to all classes of citizens** ;(...)*

great American brotherhood. I know, and I pledge my word and my
honor to the truth of the declaration, now made in this solemn presence on this grave occasion, that the white people of Louisiana, rep-
resented by the overwhelming majority of its numbers, its capital, its
intelligence, its culture, will in the administration of the government
of the State, in its executive, legislative, and judicial departments,
extend equal and impartial justice to all classes of citizens ; protect
them alike and equally in the enjoyment of all their rights of life
liberty, person, and property ; repress violence and lawlessness no
matter where it originates, or by whom committed, and thus insure
that harmony and good feeling which go hand in hand with the prog-
ress of the State in the road of happiness and prosperity.

Excerpt of congressional record-house, March 1, 1877, William M. Levy being quoted

Image from govinfo.gov

We will get back to this claim shortly.

His speech resulted in the election of Rutherford B. Hayes (see page
2068 right column).

Wherefore, I do declare--
*That **Rutherford B. Hayes**, of Ohio, having received a majority of
the whole number of electoral votes, **is duly elected President of***

__the United States for four years__, commencing on the 4th day of March, 1877.

Fast forward to 1879, William M. Levy was a member of the Louisiana State Constitutional Convention that came up with the Constitution of the State of Louisiana[28].

Article 185 second paragraph states:

He (one wanting to be able to vote) __shall be an actual resident__ of the State...

Notice that the article 187 on page 45 and 46 of that book explains the exceptions that forfeit the right for people to vote:

__Those who shall have been convicted__ of treason, embezzlement of public funds, malfeasance in office, larceny, bribery, illegal voting, or other crime punishable by hard labor or imprisonment in the penitentiary, __idiots and insane persons__.

Did the new so-called freed men own a property to be qualified as resident? Who issued the diagnosis on who was an idiot or insane? These are good questions.

The Louisiana State Museum Online[29] states that:

Once the federal government agreed to pull its troops out of Louisiana, the Nicholls administration took over. Packard's Republican supporters maintained a shadow government until the end of April 1877. A mostly Democratic convention wrote __a new constitution that voters ratified in 1879, returning Louisiana to "home rule," with white supremacist Democrats__ controlling most of the state, parish, and municipal institutions.

---

[28] *Constitution of the state of Louisiana, adopted in convention at ... New Orleans, the twenty-third day of July, A.D. 1879*, New Orleans, J.H. Cosgrove, digitized on: https://archive.org/details/constitutionsta00louigoog/page/n51/mode/2up?q=american.

[29] *LOUISIANA STATE MUSEUM ONLINE EXHIBITS THE CABILDO: TWO CENTURIES OF LOUISIANA HISTORY RECONSTRUCTION I: A STATE DIVIDED*, Louisiana Department of Culture Recreation and Tourism: https://www.crt.state.la.us/louisiana-state-museum/online-exhibits/the-cabildo/reconstruction-a-state-divided/index.

Then in 1898, the Louisiana Constitution even went further in breaking down the little gains the Black people made from the so-called liberation of 1863. We will not go into the whole history of Louisiana or the Southern States, but you can acknowledge that William M. Levy lied.

To conclude on this matter, Judah P. Benjamin[30] (so-called Jew) was the Secretary of War and State of the Confederate army and he owned plantations with dozens of slaves. He was also a prominent backer of the Ku Klux Klan. In Susan Lawrence Davis' book "Authentic History, Ku Klux Klan, 1865-1877" on page 46, she states:

Mr. Benjamin's interest in the Ku Klux Klan was so aroused that he borrowed money and gave it to Bishop Wilmer to buy horses, saddles, firearms, and other necessities for the Ku Klux Klan.

Judah P. Benjamin (1811-1884)

Image from Wikipedia

[30] Source: American Jewish Historical Society (AJHS), as reported on the Jewish Virtual Library: https://www.jewishvirtuallibrary.org/judah-benjamin.

If you don't give credit to that source, there is also the Detroit Jewish Chronicle October 9th 1925 page 6[31] which confirms his role in the Ku Klux Klan and even defends it:

The fact that Benjamin financed the Klan in 1867 cannot but speak for his good intentions and breadth of mind.
(...)
It is not by mere chance that chief among the contributors was a London Jew, Judah P. Benjamin, to whom no profits whatsoever could accrue through the operations of the Klan in the United States. In this respect, Benjamin showed himself a genuine Jew, worthy of the best Jewish traditions which call for devotion to principles of good will and loyalty that survive the strife and stress of partisan conflicts.

Article by the Detroit Jewish Chronicle October 9th, 1925

Image 1 of 3, from digital.bentley.umich.edu

The fact that Benjamin financed the Klan in 1867 cannot but speak for his good intentions and breadth of mind. This occurrence, in itself of no great importance, is of grave significance for the correct understanding of the character of the modern Ku Klux Klan in contradistinction with its predecessor of 60 years ago. In elaborating this assumption let us examine some of the data touching the origin of the modern Klan as recorded by Dr. J. M. Mecklin in his excellent book, "The Ku Klux Klan, A Study of the American Mind."

Article by the Detroit Jewish Chronicle October 9th, 1925

Image 2 of 3, from digital.bentley.umich.edu

---

[31] Herman Frank, *Judah P. Benjamin and the Ku Klux* Klan, October 9, 1925, The Detroit Jewish Chronicle, The Jewish Chronicle Publishing. Co., Inc., digitized on The Detroit Jewish News Digital Archives:
https://digital.bentley.umich.edu/djnews/djc.1925.10.09.001/6?fbclid=IwAR0Xxk9eIlWHaV0 1roH1i1j8xD2aKlp9O9H3QCw54yGp9dBP_RG9Ttejst4.

sympathizers, on the other. It is not
by mere chance that chief among the
contributors was a London Jew, Judah P. Benjamin, to whom no profits
whatsoever could accrue through the
operations of the Klan in the United
States.   In this respect, Benjamin
showed himself a genuine Jew, worthy
of the best Jewish traditions which
call for devotion to principles of good
will and loyalty that survive the strife
and stress of partisan conflicts. It is
this quality of the Jews that explains
why they have played such a conspicu-
ous part in world affairs. And it is

Article by the Detroit Jewish Chronicle October 9th, 1925

Image 3 of 3, from digital.bentley.umich.edu

Finally, here[32] is a quick example that (so-called) Jews were involved in the slave trade not only in USA, but also in Brazil (among others):

*By 1639 Dutch Brazil had a flourishing sugar industry with more than 120 sugar cane mills, six of which were owned by Jews. Jews also had an important role in commerce, tax farming, and finances. **Jews were also engaged in the slave trade**, worked in agriculture, (…)*

So, as you can see in this brief historic, the so-called Jews were involved in the slave trade and the Jim Crow Segregation. Read the books by the NOI for the sharecropping part and much more. Page 310 to 313 of Volume 2 (*Secret Relationship…*) explains the Talmudic origin of it in the book of *Bava Metzia* (although quoted *Baba Mezia*). It deals with slaves (their legal status, how to feed them, resolving a dispute between buyers and sellers) starting in chapter 8.

---

[32] *Virtual Jewish World: Recife,* Brazil, Jewish Virtual Library: https://www.jewishvirtuallibrary.org/recife-brazil.

It even states in 100b:

*Rather, Rav Sheshet said: In accordance with whose opinion is this mishna? It is Rabbi Meir, who said: **The legal status of a slave is like that of movable property**. Even if the dispute is over the slave alone, the seller can be required to take an oath.*

Or:

*With regard to slaves, he says to the victim: That which is yours is before you and no compensation is required. **Apparently, Rabbi Meir holds that the legal status of a slave is like that of land**, and not, as Rav Sheshet said, like that of movable property.*

Or 101a:

*And Rabbi Yehuda also holds that the obligation of one who receives a field of his ancestors, i.e., **a sharecropper**, <u>to pay the landowner is like that of a tenant farmer</u>, i.e., just as a tenant farmer, whether the field produces a crop or whether it does not produce a crop, is required to procure produce from somewhere, tithe it, and then give it to the landowner, as he is like one paying his debt, so too, one who receives, i.e., **a sharecropper**, <u>is also is like one paying his debt, and he must consequently first tithe the produce and then give it to the landowner</u>. **Since his obligation to the landowner is regarded as a debt, apparently before the produce is given to the landowner, it belongs to the tenant farmer or sharecropper, who is therefore required to tithe it.***

And a last example from 64b:

*The Gemara relates: Rav Yosef bar Ḥama, Rava's father, would seize the slaves of people who owed him money, and he would work them against the will of their owners. Rava, son of Rav Yosef bar Ḥama, said to him: What is the reason that the Master does this, i.e., seizes and uses these slaves? Rav Yosef bar Ḥama said to him: I maintain that the halakha is in accordance with the opinion of Rav Naḥman, **as Rav Naḥman said: <u>A slave is not worth even the bread in his stomach</u>. When the slaves work for***

me and eat in my home, I am not causing the owners any monetary loss.

I cannot finish this section without this[33]:

> *According* [to] *Professor Anita Novinsky, a specialist on the Jews at the University of Sao Paulo, "__Brazil was made by the Jews__."*

So, were the Jewish people responsible for the slave trade? We can confirm at least that they were part of it.

Jewish people conspire to control the government, the media, Hollywood, and various Black individuals and organizations

The ADL claims that:

> *Farrakhan has alleged that the Jewish people (...) conspire to control the government, the media, Hollywood, and various Black individuals and organizations.*

This claim is formulated in a hypothetical claim because of the word "conspire". Indeed, by doing so, the ADL implicitly tries to lead astray the reader that the (so-called) Jewish people do not already control the government, the media, Hollywood, various Black individuals, and organizations. Can it be proven? Yes.

<u>Control of the government</u>

In 1984, while doing a live interview[34] with Mme Sandi Freeman, she shared with her guest (Farrakhan) that (starting at 26 minutes 14 seconds):

> *I'm sorry. I've been distracted for the last 5 seconds because I've just been handed something that the Senate has just passed a resolution. And I will read to you as best I can from this copy because it is a bit difficult. "This is in the regards to the remarks, to recent statements of Louis Farrakhan. Mr. Louis Farrakhan,*

---

[33] See footnote #32.

[34] See footnote #6.

*close advisor to one of the presidential candidates has been reported to have referred to the Jewish faith as a gutter religion. Mr. Farrakhan has also accused the United States of being a criminal, for our aiding and abetting role at the time of the creation of the Israeli nation and Mr. Farrakhan has even called the very existence of Israel an outlaw act. Therefore, this is the sense of the Senate that there is no place in our society nor in our electoral process for the hateful bigoted expressions of anti-Jewish, Jewish, and racist sentiments such as those being made by Louis Farrakhan and all such vicious expressions must be condemned. **The leadership of the Senate is instructed to communicate with the chairman of the Democratic and Republican parties to request that they immediately repudiate in writing the sentiments and expressions of hatred made by Mr. Farrakhan and it was passed in the Senate moments ago 95 to 0"**.*

Isn't that a very concrete demonstration of control of the government when 95 senators out of 95 ask for the repudiation of a man telling the truth? Do notice though that the Senate got it wrong about "Jewish faith as a gutter religion". Farrakhan never said that. In the same interview, he explains he said "dirty religion" speaking of Israel, and the audio of his speech is even played proving that he never said so.

Please watch starting at 6 minutes 42 seconds and then also watch on the same video starting at 22 minutes 40 seconds and at 24 minutes 20 seconds. What he said, and his enemies put word in his mouth, was:

*Now **that nation called Israel** never had any peace in 40 years and **she will never have any peace because there can be no peace** structured on injustice, thievery, lying, and deceit and **using the name of God to shield your dirty religion under His holy and righteous Name**.*

As one can read (and hear), Judaism is not even in his quote. His enemies in a newspaper have written: "Farrakhan said Judaism is a gutter religion". They deceptively and purposely made the wrongful association of Israel with Judaism. Like he says in the interview, Israel is not Judaism. This is true. Neither is Zionism. One can claim being many things, but if the works do not bear witness to the claim, one is a liar. Does Israel follow the Torah? No. They follow the Talmud which is not the word of God revealed by inspiration to the prophet Moses.

Farrakhan explains at 23 minutes 44 seconds:

> *I could never make a statement like that and be a Muslim. **All Muslims** believe in God; believe in Moses; **believe in the Torah**; believe in the Injil brought by Jesus; and believe in the Qur'an brought by Muhammad. **How could I, in good sound mind, condemn Judaism**?*

Now that this matter has been clarified, let us keep demonstrating the control of the government by the so-called Jews.

Let us look at the list of the (so-called) Jewish members of the Congress: https://en.wikipedia.org/wiki/List_of_Jewish_members_of_the_United_States_Congress.

Let me put the most powerful lobby in the USA: https://en.wikipedia.org/wiki/Jewish_lobby. It is quite comical that the Jewish lobby entry on Wikipedia is part of a "series on antisemitism". What is more comical, yet worrying, is this:

> *When used to allege disproportionately favorable Jewish influence, it can be perceived as pejorative or as constituting antisemitism.*

I write 'comical' because in a few days, the Jewish lobby got Nick Cannon fired in July 2020 for speaking truth on <u>HIS</u> show after mentioning "Minister Farrakhan" whom they despise as a community. Who owned Viacom before it became ViacomCBS? It was the late (so-called) Jewish Sumner Murray Rothstein. ViacomCBS was founded by his daughter Shari Redstone.

Sumner Murray Rothstein (Redstone) (1923-2020)

Image from Wikipedia

Let us look at the most powerful lobby on U.S. foreign policy:

https://en.wikipedia.org/wiki/American_Israel_Public_Affairs_Committee.

And finally, let us quote from this article[35] by Jewish David J. Remnick referring to Walt and Meirsheimer's article labeled "The Israel Lobby and U.S. Foreign Policy":

> *Israel, they wrote, **has become a "strategic liability"** for the United States but retains its strong support **because of a wealthy, well-organized, <u>and bewitching lobby that has a "stranglehold" on Congress and American élites</u>**.*

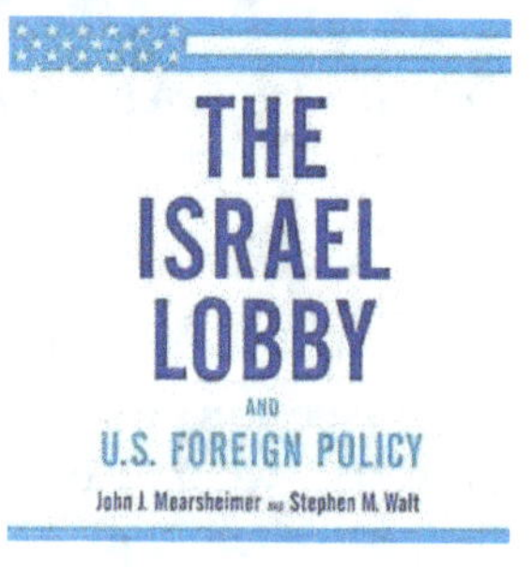

Image from Macmillian Publishers

---

[35] David Remnick, *The Lobby "The Israel Lobby and U.S. Foreign Policy"*, The New Yorker, August 27, 2007: https://www.newyorker.com/magazine/2007/09/03/the-lobby.

<u>Control of the media and Hollywood</u>

This article[36] by Manny Freidman confirms this reality.

> ***Let's be honest with ourselves, here, fellow Jews. We do control the media.*** *We've got so many dudes up in the executive offices in all the big movie production companies it's almost obscene. Just about every movie or TV show, whether it be "Tropic Thunder" ☒ or "Curb Your Enthusiasm," ☒ is rife with actors, directors, and writers who are Jewish. Did you know that all eight major film studios are run by Jews?*
>
> *But that's not all.* ***We also control the ads that go on those TV shows****.*

This comes to no surprise if you look at the list of Jewish people in the media[37] and the history of Hollywood[38]. Hollywood is controlled by the Jewish community as stated here[39] by Joel Stein.

<u>Control of various Black individuals and organizations</u>

Let's start softly with this 2018 The Hill article[40] calling for the resignation of some Black individuals from their seat as Representatives. The headline is good enough as evidence of the attempt by some of the Jewish people to control Black individuals.

> ***Jewish GOP group calls on Dem lawmakers to resign over Farrakhan remarks***

---

[36] Manny Freidman, *Jews Do Control the Media*, The Algemeiner, July 13, 2012: https://www.algemeiner.com/2012/07/03/jews-do-control-the-media/?fbclid=IwAR1ae7vYNnRXty-JzFdIWNnsvv4qDu3fBHfCCWja18gPUL0hNIaJtz81lZs.

[37] *List of Jewish American businesspeople in media*, Wikipedia: https://en.wikipedia.org/wiki/List_of_Jewish_American_businesspeople_in_media.

[38] *An Empire of Their Own*, Wikipedia: https://en.wikipedia.org/wiki/An_Empire_of_Their_Own.

[39] Who runs Hollywood? C'mon: https://www.latimes.com/archives/la-xpm-2008-dec-19-oe-stein19-story.html.

[40] Julia Manchester, *Jewish GOP group calls on Dem lawmakers to resign over Farrakhan remarks*, The Hill, March 6, 2018: https://thehill.com/blogs/blog-briefing-room/news/377053-jewish-gop-group-calls-on-lawmakers-tied-to-farrakhan-to-resign.

Let us keep building with this 1985 Chicago Tribune article[41] by Rabbi Stewart M. Weiss.

THE BLACKS MUST REPUDIATE FARRAKHAN

In this 1985 Los Angeles Times article[42], it is reported that Mayor Tom Bradley was pressured into repudiating Farrakhan.
*Jewish leaders, saying that Farrakhan has already made his anti-Jewish sentiments well known, **have been urging Bradley to repudiate Farrakhan immediately***.

And in the same article:

*Washington Mayor Marion Barry **was urged by Jewish leaders there to condemn Farrakhan <u>and did</u>** in a speech he made Monday. However, **one Jewish leader there called it "too little, too late."***

In this 1994 Washington Post article[43], we are informed that:

***Black elected officials** have long had a delicate relationship with Farrakhan. Recognizing the popularity he has with many blacks, especially the young and those in urban communities, African American politicians have been careful about criticizing Farrakhan. **Privately, some have complained about being pressured by Jewish groups to publicly repudiate comments made by Farrakhan that these groups have deemed antisemitic**.*

Even former President Barrack Obama was pressured by the ADL to "denounce Farrakhan". In this February 2018 Jewish Telegraphic Agency article[44] by Ron Kampeas, we can read that:

---

[41] Rabbi Stewart M. Weiss, *The Blacks must repudiate Farrakhan*, Chicago Tribune, December 28, 1985: https://www.chicagotribune.com/news/ct-xpm-1985-12-28-8503300345-story.html.

[42] Janet Clayton and Bill Boyarsky, *Bradley Promised Silence on Farrakhan to Black Leaders*, Los Angeles Times, September 13, 1985: https://www.latimes.com/archives/la-xpm-1985-09-13-me-22471-story.html.

[43] Kevin Merida, *BLACK LEADERS CALL ON FARRAKHAN TO REPUDIATE CONTROVERSIAL REMARKS BY AIDE*, The Washington Post, January 26, 1994: https://www.washingtonpost.com/archive/politics/1994/01/26/black-leaders-call-on-farrakhan-to-repudiate-controversial-remarks-by-aide/6c057641-c259-4803-92b2-d7fd06d27d9d/.

__The Anti-Defamation League [wants](#)[45] Obama to again denounce Farrakhan__. Attorney and pro-Israel activist Alan Dershowitz says he would not have campaigned for Obama had he known about the photo.

And lastly, since enough examples have been given concerning Black individuals being controlled or pressured by Jewish people, let us not forget Jesse Jackson who was pressured into repudiating his friend and supporter Farrakhan during his presidential campaign. In this Jewish Telegraphic Agency April 1984 [article](#)[46] by William Saphire, we can sense that pressure.

> *__Two Jewish leaders__ denounced the Black Muslim leader today for extolling Hitler and __urged Jackson again to repudiate Farrakhan__. __Rabbi Alexander Schindler__, president of the Union of American Hebrew Congregations, said, "Mr. Farrakhan has placed a storm cloud over Jesse Jackson's rainbow coalition, and the result is a dark and deeply disturbing shadow over the American political scene."*

> __Schindler added, "I pray that Rev. Jackson will use this latest wild and irresponsible statement by his supporter, Louis Farrakhan to at last publicly dissociate himself from Mr. Farrakhan and the dangerous demagogy he represents.__"

---

[44] Ron Kampeas, *What was Louis Farrakhan doing at that Congressional Black Caucus meeting with Obama? Here's what we found out*, Jewish Telegraphic Agency, February 1, 2019: https://www.jta.org/2018/02/01/politics/what-was-louis-farrakhan-doing-at-a-congressional-black-caucus-meeting.

[45] *ADL head calls on Barack Obama to again denounce Louis Farrakhan*, Jewish Telegraphic Agency, January 31, 2018: https://www.jta.org/2018/01/31/united-states/adl-head-calls-on-barack-obama-to-again-denounce-louis-farrakhan.

[46] William Saphire, *BLACK MUSLIM LEADER EXTOLS HITLER*, Daily News Bulletin, Published by Jewish Telegraphic Agency, April 13, 1984: http://pdfs.jta.org/1984/1984-04-13_072.pdf?_ga=2.22030331.1582539831.1598758837-1241064722.1595383865.

Evidently, the pressure got the best of Reverend Jesse Jackson because in June 1984, he distanced himself from his friend and supporter as we can read in this article[47].

> *"I will not permit Minister Farrakhan's words, wittingly or unwittingly, to divide the Democratic Party," he said, asserting that the Muslim leader "is not a part of our campaign."*
> *(...)*
> ***Mr. Jackson's statement was issued amid mounting pressure on him to repudiate Mr. Farrakhan and his statements*** *and on Walter F. Mondale, the apparent Democratic Presidential nominee, to repudiate Mr. Jackson for his continued association with the Chicago-based Muslim leader.*

So, the fact that Jewish people do indeed control Black individuals has been demonstrated. What about Black organizations?

This Los Angeles Times October 1993 article[48] by Kenneth Reich and Richard C. Paddock goes along that narrative.

> *An array of civil rights organizations filed a federal lawsuit Thursday against the Anti-Defamation League and law enforcement authorities in Los Angeles, San Francisco, and San Diego, **asking for an injunction against spying and damages for alleged privacy violations**.*
>
> ***Groups representing Arab-Americans and African Americans led the effort**, along with other organizations. Joining in the suit were former Lt. Gov. Mervyn Dymally, former Los Angeles City Councilman Robert Farrell and others who said their names turned up in files obtained by ADL operatives from police agencies.*

---

[47] Fay S. Joyce, *Jackson Criticizes Remarks Made By Farrakhan As 'Reprehensible'*, The New York Times, June 29, 1984: https://www.nytimes.com/1984/06/29/world/jackson-criticizes-remarks-made-by-farrakhan-as-reprehensible.html.

[48] Kenneth Reich and Richard C. Paddock, *Civil Rights Groups Sue ADL, Ask for Injunction Against Spying : Court: Plaintiffs say that law enforcement authorities allowed confidential files to be given to the Jewish anti-extremism organization*, Los Angeles Times, October 22, 1993: https://www.latimes.com/archives/la-xpm-1993-10-22-me-48538-story.html.

How better to control an organization than to be either a financial contributor or the chairman or even the president?

The NAACP idea started with Mary White Ovington, William English Walling and Henry Moskowitz[49]. Then, Joel Spingarn[50] became chairman in 1914 and, according to Jewish historian Howard M. Sachar, brought in other Jews[51] in its ranks such as: Jacob Schiff, Jacob Billikopf, and Rabbi Stephen Wise. He later became treasurer and the second president of that organization. He also had his brother Arthur[52] in the NAACP heading the legal committee and then president after his brother's death. The interesting part about the NAACP is that the president, Joel, was a critic[53] of Booker T. Washington who promoted the economic independence of the so-called Negro. Notice that they also went, while still under the leadership of Spingarn, against[54] the great Marcus Garvey[55] who was also about Black independence both economically and as a Nation. Notice that the article only mentions W.E.B. Du Bois and the rivalry between the organization and Mr. Garvey's Universal Negro Improvement Association. It is also worthy of mention that both Booker T. Washington and Marcus Garvey had the same ideology foundation for a successful uplifting of the Black community: economic independence, while the NAACP's foundation was integration into White's economy. So here we have so-called Jews in control of an organization that allegedly promotes civil rights for Blacks but consider Black leaders promoting economic independence as rivals and even complain when they are successful in gathering property.

---

[49] *Henry Moskowitz*, Wikipedia: https://en.wikipedia.org/wiki/Henry_Moskowitz_(activist).

[50] *Joel* Spingarn, the Jewish Virtual Library: https://www.jewishvirtuallibrary.org/joel-spingarn.

[51] Howard Sachar, *Jews in the Civil Rights Movement*, My Jewish Learnings: https://www.myjewishlearning.com/article/jews-in-the-civil-rights-movement/.

[52] *Arthur B. Spingarn*, Wikipedia: https://en.wikipedia.org/wiki/Arthur_B._Spingarn.

[53] *Joel Spingarn attacks Dr. Washington*, The New York Age, February 26, 1914, Newspapers: https://www.newspapers.com/clip/25865880/spingarn-attacks-booker-t-washington/.

[54] *Interference with the Universal Negro Improvement Association*, NAACP: A Century in the Fight for Freedom, Library of Congress: www.loc.gov/exhibits/naacp/the-new-negro-movement.html#obj11.

[55] *Interference with the Universal Negro Improvement Association*, NAACP: A Century in the Fight for Freedom, Library of Congress: www.loc.gov/exhibits/naacp/the-new-negro-movement.html#obj10.

Joel Spingarn (1875-1939)

Image from Wikipedia

Let us fast forward to 2020 and the NAACP is still under Jewish control. Indeed, not only they called for the removal of Philadelphia's NAACP president, Rodney Muhammad[56], over a single cartoon posted on social media, but they were successful in having him removed. The organization even went as far as voting to "effectively dissolve itself and yield full control of the national office[57]" under Jewish pressure. Isn't that the very definition of controlling Black organizations?

But what about the Simon Wiesenthal Center pressuring[58] Black organizations (Fox Soul TV and Revolt TV) into not airing

---

[56] Stephan Salisbury, *Jewish groups call for ouster of local NAACP head over anti-Semitic Facebook post*, The Philadelphia Inquirer, July 25, 2020: https://www.inquirer.com/news/rodney-muhammad-naacp-anti-semitic-jewish-federation-adl-20200725.html.

[57] Michael D'Onofrio, *National NAACP takes over Philly chapter after president's anti-Semitic Facebook post*, The Philadelphia Tribune, August 26, 2020: https://www.phillytrib.com/news/local_news/national-naacp-takes-over-philadelphia-chapter-after-presidents-anti-semitic-facebook-post/article_068d7cf9-2fb3-5562-b893-0b497fc6bde7.html.

[58] Jerusalem Post Staff, *Simon Wiesenthal Center condemns Farrakhan's July 4th speech on Revolt TV*, The Jerusalem Post, July 6, 2020: https://www.jpost.com/diaspora/antisemitism/simon-wiesenthal-center-condemns-farrakhans-july-4th-speech-on-revolt-tv-634010?fbclid=IwAR1MAkpHR6aqlTVtSWBiQHkTE1ZQMCsAWFR0OqztUqc5hU3VJsxiGrmx7i0.

Farrakhan's 4th of July, 2020, message to the world? Fox Soul TV bended under the pressure, but Revolt TV did not. So, what happened? The Jewish people went to work to get the speech successfully removed from YouTube[59].

<u>The FBI and ADL's liaison can't be overlooked</u>

It is a known fact that the FBI (founded in 1908) is an enemy to Black advancement.

The FBI's agents of the Counterintelligence Program (COINTELPRO) have worked relentlessly to destroy any black organization that would uplift the Black community from its state of mental and economic death deeming them as hate-type. Even the peaceful ones like Dr. Martin Luther King jr. This is well-known since **The Church Committee Report of 1976** which is a massive investigation on the operations of US agencies such as the FBI.

The Nation of Islam's website has some of the COINTELPRO documents here: https://www.noi.org/cointelpro/[60].

This 1967 document https://www.noi.org/fbi_08-25-1967/[61] states:

> ***The purpose of this new counterintelligence endeavor is to expose, disrupt, misdirect, discredit, or otherwise <u>neutralize the activities of black nationalist</u>, hate-type organizations and groupings, their leadership, spokesmen, membership, and supporters, and to counter their propensity for violence and civil disorder. The activities of all such groups of intelligence interest to this Bureau must be followed on a continuous basis so we will be in position to promptly take advantage of all opportunities for***

---

[59] Askia Muhammad, *MUHAMMAD: The Censorship of Louis Farrakhan*, The Washington Informer, July 15, 2020: https://www.washingtoninformer.com/muhammad-the-censorship-of-louis-farrakhan/.

[60] *FBI COINTELPRO: The U.S. Government's War Against Dissent*, The Nation of Islam: https://www.noi.org/cointelpro/.

[61] *FBI COINTELPRO: The U.S. Government's War Against Dissent*, The Nation of Islam: https://www.noi.org/fbi_08-25-1967/.

counterintelligence and to inspire action in instances where circumstances warrant. The pernicious background of such groups, their duplicity, and devious maneuvers must be exposed to public scrutiny where such publicity will have a neutralizing effect. **Efforts of various groups to consolidate their forces or to recruit new or youthful adherents must be frustrated.**

This 1967 file from The Church Committee even proves that one of the COINTELPRO's goals was to prevent the rise of a Messiah[62].

2. **prevent the rise of a "messiah" who could unify, and electrify, the militant black nationalist movement.** *(Censored) might have been such a "messiah;" he is the martyr of the movement today. (...)*

```
              2.  Prevent the rise of a "messiah" who could
unify, and electrify, the militant black nationalist movement.
             might have been such a "messiah;" he is the martyr
of the movement today.
and                       all aspire to this position.
             is less of a threat because of his age.         could
be a very real contender for this position should he abandon
his supposed "obedience" to "white, liberal doctrines"
(nonviolence) and embrace black nationalism.
has the necessary charisma to be a real threat in this way.

    3    Prevent  'violence
```

Excerpt from declassified documents of the FBI COINTEL Program

Image from aarclibrary.org

We can tell by the end of the paragraph that they are referring to Malcom X, then to Elijah Muhammad and Dr. Martin Luther King Jr.

So knowing this, let's go back to this 1993 Los Angeles Times article[63] previously mentioned and written by Kenneth Reich and Richard C. Paddock: *Civil Rights Groups Sue ADL, Ask for Injunction Against Spying : Court: Plaintiffs say that law*

---

[62] *Volume 6: Federal Bureau of Investigation,* Assassination Archives and Research Center: https://www.aarclibrary.org/publib/church/reports/vol6/html/ChurchV6_0200a.htm.

[63] See footnote #48.

enforcement authorities allowed confidential files to be given to the Jewish anti-extremism organization.

The article mentions "law enforcement authorities". On this website[64], the liaison is proven a reality between the ADL and the FBI. In 1968, the Director of the Bureau orders all field offices to establish liaisons with the ADL[65].

```
Director, FBI                                    1/25/68


SAC, Indianapolis  (100-16164)  (RUC)


LIAISON WITH THE ANTI-DEFAMATION
LEAGUE OF B'NAI B'RITH
INFORMATION CONCERNING
(INTERNAL SECURITY)


        ReBuairtel 1/17/68.

            Indianapolis has had liaison with Anti-Defamation      b6
League, Indiana, for past ten years. [            ] Indiana        b7C
Regional Office Director, as well as his office staff, have
been most cooperative with this office on all matters.
```

Image from israellobby.org

Incidentally, the ADL seems to have been spying, or at least monitoring, Black organizations. In 1992, they published a report called: The Anti-Semitism of Black Demagogues and Extremists[66] (starting at page 20 of 92).

---

[64] *The FBI and the Anti-Defamation League*, The Israel Lobby Archive – The Institute for Research: Middle Eastern Policy: https://www.israellobby.org/ADL/.

[65] The Israel Lobby Archive – The Institute for Research: Middle Eastern Policy: https://www.israellobby.org/ADL/1199215-000%20---%20100-IP-16164%20---%20Section%201.PDF.

[66] The Israel Lobby Archive – The Institute for Research: Middle Eastern Policy: https://www.israellobby.org/ADL/1199215-000%20---%2044B-LA-145408%20---%20Section%201.PDF.

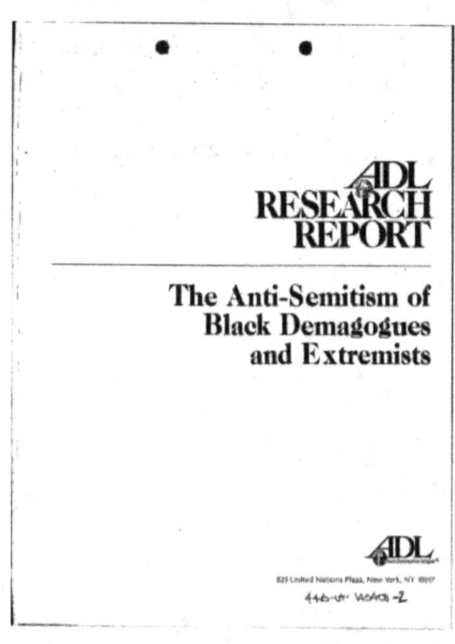

Image from israellobby.org (page 20/92)

We can see that the ADL's biggest interest (or obsession) is Farrakhan and the Nation of Islam. It also shows the ADL's interest in Black student groups on campus.

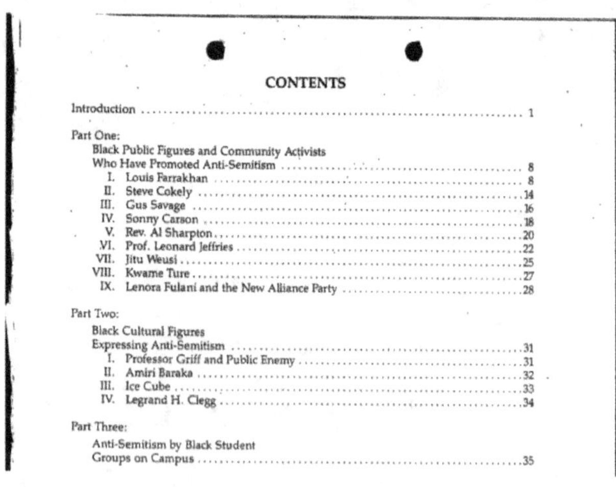

CONTENTS

Image from israellobby.org (page 21/92)

It is a known fact that the Jewish community has put pressure on campuses to prevent Farrakhan or the Nation of Islam in giving speeches through their medias. Here[67] is an example from 1984, here[68] from 1987, here[69] from 1988 and here[70] from 2014.

Their tactics to try to remove the magnetism of Farrakhan seem to be a carbon copy of the COINTEL Program, doesn't it?

Denying Jews a legitimate claim to Judaism and the land called Israel

The ADL claims:

> *He also frequently denies that Jews have a legitimate claim to their religion and to the land of Israel…*

Again, no sources are offered to back their claim. So, let us assume that it cannot be attributed to Farrakhan. Can we nevertheless say something about their claim?

Well, what is the religion of Jews in the first place? We already demonstrated that there are Jews who follow the Torah (or Old Testament) and those who follow the Talmud (a fabricated interpretation of the Torah that supersedes it). The word "Jew" does not appear in the Bible before long _after_ the Pentateuch. So, this tells us many things. One of which, Moses is not a Jew and therefore, did not teach "Judaism". If we break down the word "Judaism", we have the name Judah or Judea. Judah and Judea were not there when

---

[67] Jeffrey Schmalz, *Invitation to Farrakhan Causes Rift at Wesleyan*, The New York Times, October 9, 1984: https://www.nytimes.com/1984/10/09/nyregion/invitation-to-farrakhan-causes-rift-at-wesleyan.html.

[68] AP, *Syracuse Group Refuses to Cut Off Funds for Farrakhan Talk*, The New York Times, November 8, 1987: https://www.nytimes.com/1987/11/08/nyregion/syracuse-group-refuses-to-cut-off-funds-for-farrakhan-talk.html.

[69] William K. Stevens, *In Tense Times at Penn, Enter Farrakhan*, The New York Times, April 11, 1988: https://www.nytimes.com/1988/04/11/us/in-tense-times-at-penn-enter-farrakhan.html.

[70] Jay Bernstein, *Morgan leadership must denounce Farrakhan's appearance*, The Baltimore Sun, November 19, 2014: https://www.baltimoresun.com/opinion/op-ed/bs-ed-farrakhan-morgan-20141119-story.html.

Abraham was receiving the Lord in his tent (Genesis chapter 18, verse 1).

So, Moses taught something other than Judaism. He taught the same as the prophets before him: complete submission to the will of the One God (Allah). In other words, he taught Islam.

Knowing that the Holy Land was populated by Black people until quite recently (less than 6000 years), it is unconceivable that White people claiming the religion of Judaism have anything to do with the land of the Fertile Crescent and to the promise by God to Abraham. Abraham lived in what is now called Saudi Arabia. So, White Jews had to be taught by someone and that teaching would later be known as "Judaism". The Jews are correct in that Moses came to them. As Elijah Muhammad teaches in his *Message to the Blackman in America* on page 120 about White people being expelled to Europe from the Holy Land:

> *"After 2,000 years of living as a savage, Allah raised up Musa (Moses) to bring the white race again into civilization: to take their place as rulers, as Yakub had intended for them. Musa (Moses) became their God and leader. He brought out of the caves; taught them to believe in Allah; taught them to wear clothes; how to cook their food; how to season it with salt; what beef they should kill and eat; and, how to use fire for their service. Moses taught them against putting the female cow under burden."*

Image from the Final Call Store

This article[71] confirms that Ashkenazim have no roots in Palestine. It states to no one's surprise:

*Though the finding may seem intuitive, it contradicts the notion that European Jews mostly descend from people who left Israel and the Middle East around 2,000 years ago. **Instead, a substantial proportion of the population originates from local Europeans who converted to Judaism, said study co-author Martin Richards, an Archaeogeneticist at the University of Huddersfield in England**.*

This was figured out by Ashkenazi Jew Arthur Koestler and put into a book he wrote called "*The Thirteenth Tribe*: *The Khazar Empire and Its Heritage*" (1976) which can be found online here[72]. It goes as far as telling that today's Jews are only converts. If Black people would claim to be the real Jews (actually Hebrews) they would be justified in making that claim. How is that so: because to be a convert you need to have a teacher. This is explained in the Bible in the book of John chapter 3, verse 14:

And as Moses lifted up the serpent in the wilderness, *even so must the Son of man be lifted up:*

Was Europe a wilderness 4,000 years ago? More likely than otherwise.

---

[71] Tia Ghose, *Surprise: Ashkenazi Jews Are Genetically European*, Live Science, October 8, 2013: https://www.livescience.com/40247-ashkenazi-jews-have-european-genes.html.

[72] Arthur Koestler, *The Thirteenth Tribe*, Fantompowa: http://www.fantompowa.info/13th%20Tribe.pdf.

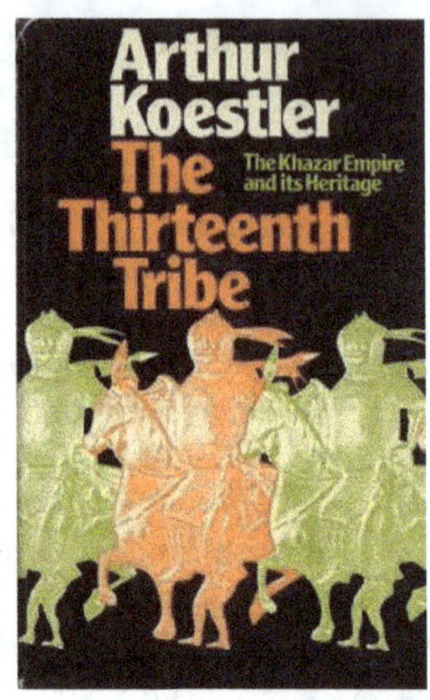

Image from Wikipedia

White people, in homage to Moses, even have his statue at the Library of Congress[73].

Statue of Moses at the Library of Congress

Image from Wikipedia

---

[73] *File: Moses LOC.jpg*, Wikipedia: https://en.wikipedia.org/wiki/File:Moses_LOC.jpg.

So, to sum up about the legitimacy of their claim to Islam (what Moses practiced), they factually cannot claim it as their own because Islam existed since the Creation. There was just not a necessity to give it a name (Islam) up until Prophet Muhammad walked the earth. On the other side, some Jews can claim the religion that came out of the Talmud. However, the Talmud does not give them legitimacy to the Holy Land. So, when Jewish Germans and Poles invaded Palestine in the 1900s, they had no legitimate claim to that part of the Earth. If we go further, White people have no claim of any land on the planet other than what they are allowed by Black people because they (Whites) just arrived here 6,000 years ago.

Claiming that Judaism is nothing more than a "deceptive lie" and a "theological error"

The ADL claims Farrakhan says or said:

> ... *Judaism is nothing more than a "deceptive lie" and a "theological error" promoted by Jews to further their supposed control over America's government and economy.*

As usual, no sources to confirm if what the ADL claims have been said by Farrakhan actually happened. Hence, they once again believe we can accept their claim at face value. Referring to Judaism as a "deceptive lie" and a "theological error" does not go along with what can be proven Farrakhan said about Judaism.

For instance, in 1984, in the interview[74] with Mme Sandi Freeman referred previously in the analysis, Farrakhan explains the lie of "Judaism being a gutter religion", starting at 23 minutes 44 seconds that:

> *I could never make a statement like that and be a Muslim. **All Muslims** believe in God; believe in Moses; **believe in the Torah**; believe in the Injil brought by Jesus; and believe in the Qur'an brought by Muhammad. **How could I, in good sound mind, condemn Judaism**?*

---

[74] See footnote #6.

Does that factual and traceable statement corroborate the claim by the ADL? The answer is evidently: no.

So, what about the "theological error"? It is not Judaism that is a theological error but people who would attribute the Promised Land by God to Abraham (a Black man) as belonging to a community (White Jews) that did not even exist when such promise was made.

Remember now, Jews are not in the Pentateuch which came with Moses way after the death of Prophet Abraham. So, to claim a land based on a religion learned from another community is as foolish as me being taught Buddhism and then go to China and remove people from their land saying that it belongs to me. Well, the State of Israel has done that in front of the whole world.

Do Germans, Poles and Russians have any connection with Palestine? The answer is self-evident.

The role of Israel and the Jews in orchestrating the 9/11 attacks and Israel and Jews don't fear America because they control if from within

The ADL claims, and finally gives a reference, that:

> *During Part 2 of his 2015 Saviours' Day keynote address at the Mosque Maryam in Chicago, Illinois, Farrakhan used his platform to discuss the supposed role of Israel and Jews in orchestrating the 9/11 attacks, claiming that "Israelis had foreknowledge of the attacks" and that Jews were warned ahead of time not to come to work that day. He then went on to speak more broadly of Israeli control of the American government, stating that Israel and Jews "don't fear America because they control it from within."*

The lecture can be bought here[75] at the Final Call Store as a CD or DVD.

The ADL certainly needs to learn how to quote Farrakhan. Let us start with the end of their claim since it is the shortest to analyze. They say: "… Israel and Jews "don't fear America because they control it from within."

Here is the real quote starting at 1 hour 11 minutes 30 seconds:

> *Before Netanyahu, **Ariel Sharon**, the former Prime minister that died recently, was in a debate with his foreign minister Shimon Peres. When **Sharon** reportedly yelled, quote: **"Don't worry about American pressure. We, the Jewish people, control America!"***

---

[75] *Saviours' Day 2015 Pt2: The Intensifying Universal Cry for Justice*, March 1, 2015, The Final Call Online Store: https://finalcallstore.noi.org/product/saviours-day-2015-pt-2-the-intensifying-universal-cry-for-justice-dvd/.

So, he was quoting Ariel Sharon. The demonstration of that control has been demonstrated previously in this analysis, so no need to repeat myself here.

Farrakhan states starting at 1 hour 41 minutes and 33 seconds:

Thanks to the exemplary work of scholars like Victor Thorn and Christopher Bollyn, it is now becoming apparent that there were many Israelis and Zionist Jews in key roles in the 9/11 attacks. Now look, if they can prove me wrong, like I said, I'll pay with my life. Since they want to kill me anyway, prove me wrong! We're dealing with thieves and liars and murderers. Listen to this.

We know that many Israelis were arrested immediately after attacks but quickly released and sent to Israel. We know that the World Trade Center building was insured by its owner, Larry Silverstein, right before the attack and in the insurance clause, or there was a clause, that if the building were damaged by terrorist acts, Mr. Silverstein would get paid. And guess what? Mr. Silverstein got 4.8 billion dollars.

We know that an Israeli film crew dressed as Arabs were fil... filming the Twin Towers before the first plane went in. In other words, these Israelis had foreknowledge of the attacks. Now look! You say: "But planes went into these towers." Yes, they did. But do you know what kind of technology you'd have to have as a pilot to fly a plane and drop down to an altitude and turn at an angle at 4 or 5 hundred miles an hour into a building? And the fuel of an airplane is not strong enough to create enough heat to melt the steel structure of that building.

We know that many Jews received the text message not to come to work on September 11. Who sent that message that kept them from showing up?

Within minutes of the attacks, Ehud Barak, the founder, and master of the Israeli military's covert operation force was in a

*London studio of the BBC blaming Osama Bin Laden and calling
for a war on terror[76].*

*And we know that Benjamin Netanyahu told an audience in
Israel[77]: "we are benefiting from one thing. And that is the attack
on the Twin towers and Pentagon and the American struggle in
Iraq." He added that these catastrophes and wars would swing
the American public opinion in the favor of Israel.*

Fox News made a four parts coverage[78] on an Israeli spy ring in USA
that knew 9/11 was on the making.

Image from YouTube

In it, we learn how aggressively the Israelis spy on their so-called
friend the USA. We also learn that, at least at that time, all phone call
records and billing in the U.S. were done by Amdocs Limited. An
Israeli based private telecommunication company. The Israelis
claimed it is to prevent fraud while the U.S. Counterintelligence

---

[76] *Ehud Barak Is Real Terrorist - BBC Interview - Date 9/11/2001*, YouTube:
https://www.youtube.com/watch?v=TFEgBCrBb1Y.

[77] *Report: Netanyahu Says 9/11 Terror Attacks Good for Israel*, Haaretz, April 16, 2008:
https://www.haaretz.com/1.4970678.

[78] *Fox News: Israeli Spy Ring Operating In America*, YouTube:
https://www.youtube.com/watch?v=9J-eAtxX7l0

analysts say it could also be used to spy through the phone system. The anchor states starting at 9 minutes 31 seconds:

> **There was a report**, *you recall*, **that the MOSSAD, the Israeli Intelligence Agency, did indeed send representatives in the U.S. to warn just before 9/11 that a major terrorist attack was imminent**. *Why does that not… how does that leave room for a lack of a warning?*

This, by the way, contradicts Ehud Barak in his 9/11 interview on BBC mentioned previously.

Ehud Barak

Image from Wikipedia

We also learn from the coverage that "Comverse InfoSys[79], a subsidiary of **an Israeli run private telecommunications firm** with offices throughout the U.S. **It provides wiretapping equipment for law enforcement**." Those computers "intercept, record and store the wiretapped calls" and Israel still has continuing access to it with the claim it is to keep them free of glitches. The coverage goes on to explain the vulnerability of the Israeli technology and how it could be used by Israel and that the company works closely with the Israeli government.

---

[79] *Converse Technology*, Wikipedia: https://en.wikipedia.org/wiki/Comverse_Technology.

The News anchor asks the obvious question: "Is there any reason to suspect in this instance that the Israeli government is involved?" To which reporter Carl Cameron answers:

> *No there's not. But there are growing instincts and an awful lot of* **law enforcement officials and a variety of agencies who suspect that and have begun compiling evidence**. *And a highly classified investigation and think precisely that possibility.*

It is interesting that the coverage gives all the indication of the involvement of Israel in the 9/11 attacks but then claims there's no reason to suspect that. Furthermore, we are supposed to believe the Israelis were spying on the "evil" Arabs although once the law enforcement started to investigate on them, Israelis were returning to or being returned to Israel. Indeed, freelance journalist and author Christopher Ketcham reported in his May 2002 article *The Israeli "art student" mystery*[80] that in between March 2001 and September 11, 2001: "… some 140 Israeli nationals were detained or arrested." He also reports:

> *According to the INS, the deportations resulted from violations of student visas that forbade the Israelis from working in the United States.* **(In fact, Salon has established that none of the Israelis were enrolled in the art school most of them claimed to be attending; the other college they claimed to be enrolled in does not exist.)** *After the Sept. 11 attacks, many more young Israelis -- 60, according to one AP dispatch and other reports -- were detained and deported.*

Of those Israelis, 5 of them were caught by the police on that terrible day with explosives and Arab outfits in their van. It has been reported[81] that a woman had seen them celebrating while the towers were on fire. They were labeled "the 5 dancing Israelis" and claimed to be working for the New-Jersey-based Urban Moving Systems

---

[80] Christopher Ketcham, *The Israeli "art student" mystery*, Salon, May 7, 2002: https://www.salon.com/2002/05/07/students/.

[81] *Were Israelis Detained on Sept. 11 Spies?*, ABC NEWS, January 6, 2006: https://abcnews.go.com/2020/story?id=123885&page=1.

Company. When they went back to Israel, one of them said on national television "we were there to document[82]" the event.

But how did they know it was going to happen unless Israel was involved?

The 5 dancing Israelis during the 9/11 attacks in New York, 2001

Image from YouTube

Interestingly enough, one of the two police officers, former policeman Scott DeCarlo now musician and singer, who arrested these Israelis, did an interview[83] in 2011 with Dave Gahary about the event and what he could remember of it. Despite believing not having done much other than arrest a few men, his testimony of the event has much relevance to the issue. Here is the transcription of parts of the interview.

> *D. G.: Okay. It was him and it was a couple of other guys. It was a total of five of them?*
>
> *S.D.: Correct. Yeah.*
>
> *D.G.: Did you have any idea at that time the nationality of these men?*

---

[82] *5 dancing Israelis*, YouTube: https://www.youtube.com/watch?v=yLnKiTmO64c.

[83] American Free Press: https://americanfreepress.net/9-11-cop-who-arrested-dancing-israelis-speaks/.

*S.D.: No sir. But when removed them, I forget which guy it was. Kind of chatty but: "**Hey, we're not your enemy or your friend. Our enemies are your enemies**" or whatever at that point. They said they were from Israel or something and I don't remember exactly what they said. But there was something along them lines.*

Let's keep digging the Israeli "coincidences."

Two of Odigo Messenger's workers received messages 2 hours before the terrorist attacks. The article[84] states:

> *Micha Macover, CEO of the company, **said the two workers received the messages and immediately after the terror attack informed the company's management**, which immediately contacted the Israeli security services, which brought in the FBI.*

This foreknowledge of the attacks is what reinforced the claim of some people that most Jews did not show up at the WTC that day. The Jerusalem Post mentioned on September 12th that 4 000 Israelis were missing[85] in the area of the WTC according to the Israeli government. The headline might have been misinterpreted by many people that some people did not show up because of the foreknowledge of the attacks. The counter-argument[86] of it being just a rumor that 4000 did not show up is that Jews did indeed die in that attack. But that argument does not negate the Odigo event or the Fox News coverage of the Israeli spy ring or the MOSSAD being sent on the USA to warn of an upcoming attack.

And finally, about 9/11, another issue pointing at Israeli involvement, Larry Silverstein (so-called Jew) bought the WTC and

---

[84] Yuval Dror, *Odigo Says Workers Were Warned of Attack*, Haaretz, September 26, 2001: https://www.haaretz.com/1.5410231.

[85] *Hundreds of Israelis missing in WTC attack*, The Internet Jerusalem Post, September 12, 2001 Internet Archive Wayback Machine: https://web.archive.org/web/20050412040213/http:/www.fpp.co.uk/online/02/10/JerusPost120901.html.

[86] *The 4,000 Jews Rumor*, International Information Programs, Internet Archive Wayback Machine: https://web.archive.org/web/20050408072925/http:/usinfo.state.gov/media/Archive/2005/Jan/14-260933.html.

got an insurance policy a few weeks prior to the attacks against terrorist attacks and collected on both towers. How did he know to buy them and get insurance for those types of event? He is also <u>a known friend of Benjamin Netanyahu</u>[87].

Larry Silverstein

Image from Wikipedia

Since many media platforms are mostly owned by (so-called) Jews, who still promote all over the world the lie about the towers collapsing at free-fall due to fire, despite the evidence it was a controlled demolition. We must assume that the (so-called) Jewish lobby has influence all over the world. The fire theory to explain less than 12 seconds of collapsing for both towers and <u>most of all of Building #7</u> is laughable. We are to believe that the steel got weak enough because the fire was so intense, but human beings were able to reach the windows despite that 'infernal' heat as if flesh were more resistant than steel. I am not going to elaborate any more because the point being made is the Israeli involvement, not how/what happened.

This is not the first time Zionist Jews tried to blame Arabs or darker people for their own terrorist attacks. Do you remember the King David Hotel terrorist attack by the Irgun (yes, the same terrorist group mentioned earlier in which Rahm Emanuel's father was a part of)? Weren't the perpetrators disguised as Arabs but due to their

---

[87] Sara Leibovich-Dar, *Up in Smoke*, Haaretz, November 21, 2001: https://www.haaretz.com/1.5462012.

incompetence, they got caught by the British? They were even proud of such terrorist attack! Let us have a look.

Listen very carefully to terrorist Izahk Zadok recalling of events starting at 3 minutes 34 seconds in this historical video[88]:

*There were lots of people around in the corridor. We tried to move them out of the way: here, there, to the side. But there were some who resisted. But we threatened them with our weapons. **I wasn't dressed as a civilian or a soldier. I was dressed like an Arab** with the jalabiya and the keffiyeh... with that ring on your head. You know like... oh what's he called... the leader of the Arabs. You know? Arafat.*

Izahk Zadok

Image from YouTube

As if making a false flag terrorist attack was not low down enough, they claimed that they did not want anyone to die (91 deaths of which **17 Jews**, 41 Arabs) from their terrorist attack or have it aimed at civilian targets. The British Chief Secretary in Palestine, Sir Henry Gurney, wrote, according to the documentary, that he had witnessed a deliberate and indiscriminately Irgun attack on civilians to create panic among the population. We will get back later to why I emphasize the number of Jews killed.

---

[88] *1946 King David Hotel Bombing*, YouTube: https://www.youtube.com/watch?v=7lFayd9TWa0.

In this <u>video</u>[89], terrorist and former Prime Minister of Israel Menachem Begin puts forth a beautiful lie immediately refuted by Chief Secretary John Shaw of the Government of Palestine:

> *We did not even imagine that one life would be lost*. **We did our best to ensure that everyone would be evacuated from the King David Hotel**. *Everything was coordinated between the operation officer Haganah (paramilitary organization) and our own. The timing… the warning… which was giving in advance. The explosion occurred just as we have planned it. About half an hour of the telephone warning was given. There were 3 warnings by telephone*. **The British did not heed our warning**.

This example of a failed false flag attack should give you the hint that Zionist (so-called) Jews do not care about the loss of Jewish lives as long as their objective is fulfilled.

That is why I emphasized the 17 Jewish victims. And maybe you already have forgotten that I have mentioned earlier that some Zionists (so-called) Jews collaborated with the Nazis and were against the rescue of their brethren in Europe. Less than a thousand Jews for the destruction of the Middle East might be a small price to pay by the Zionists compared to WW2.

What was the result of 9/11? The war on Islam and not the war on terrorism.

---

[89] *Palestine 1946: King David Hotel Bomb Warning Controversy*, YouTube: https://www.youtube.com/watch?v=4ZHHTjuv5jc.

Section 4 - Page 1, paragraph 4 of the ADL's report

Farrakhan likened himself to Henry Ford and calls him a great man and says he's in good company

The ADL writes about Saviours' Day 2014[90]:

> *... Farrakhan likened himself to auto magnate Henry Ford, who promoted anti-Semitic conspiracies in the 1920s in The International Jew: The World's Foremost Problem. Farrakhan called Ford "a great man who was called an anti-Semite" and added, "I feel like I'm in good company."*

The ADL tries deceitfully to claim that he compared himself to Ford because of their alleged "anti-Semitism". First of all, Farrakhan did not compare himself to Henry Ford in any way. While speaking of the importance of the city of Detroit in the economy of the USA, he said, starting at 1 hour 6 minutes 37 seconds:

> *This city gave economic life and stability to America and made her a power through the automobile industry throughout the world. Detroit attracted Black people from the South who were tired of sharecropping and allowing somebody else to take advantage of their sweat and their labor and they came to Detroit seeking a job. And they started working in these factories. **Mr. Ford, a great man, who was called an anti-Semite[91] ... no I feel like I'm in good company**. That man set up in Highland Park, a community building homes for the workers to give them a middle-class existence. And there was a time in Detroit when Black people in Detroit were living under the best housing conditions of any city in America.*

---

[90] *How Strong Is Our Foundation; Can We Survive? – Saviours' Day 2014*, The Final Call Online Store: https://finalcallstore.noi.org/product/how-strong-is-our-foundation-can-we-survive-saviours-day-2014-dvd/.

[91] Victoria Saker, *Why Ford needs to grapple with its founder's anti-Semitism*, The Washington Post, February 9, 2019: https://www.washingtonpost.com/outlook/2019/02/08/why-ford-needs-grapple-with-its-founders-anti-semitism/.

Henry Ford (1863-1947)

Image form Wikipedia

Secondly, there is no problem with saying Henry Ford was a great man, since he revolutionized the automobile industry, but also because even the Jewish Virtual Library[92] calls him an "industrial genius", a "true giant" and "great man". So, he was, and still is, called an anti-Semite and considered great.

So, the ADL accuses Farrakhan of something that is confirmed by the Jewish Virtual Library. Then, the ADL states:

*In Part 2 of his Saviours' Day address at Mosque Maryam in Chicago, Farrakhan received a standing ovation after telling his audience that **"the Satanic Jews that control everything and mostly everybody, if they are your enemy, then you must be somebody."***

This is an example why the ADL cannot be trusted for reporting basically anything. If they lie with quotes and details, the credibility falls flat. Let me quote you what was said and most importantly why the people in the Mosque gave a standing ovation. Here is what

---

[92] *Anti-Semitism in the United States: Henry Ford Invents a Jewish Conspiracy*, Jewish Virtual Library: https://www.jewishvirtuallibrary.org/henry-ford-invents-a-jewish-conspiracy.

Farrakhan said starting at 11 minutes 48 seconds of the CD available here[93] for only 2 dollars:

> *How do you measure strength? The strength of a thing is measured by its ability to withstand great force or pressure. Some say: "Farrakhan, you're a strong man." Why do you say that?*
>
> *I went to buy a pair of shoes yesterday and the man was so happy that I came in his store. He said to me. He said: "brother, I wanted to give you a pair of shoes." He said: "because you've been out there taking all the breaks for us."*
>
> *I thought about what he said. See, you can tell who a man is by measuring his enemies. See if your enemies are little punks out there, you ain't nothing! I mean, he's a little so. <u>But if your enemy is the government of the United States of America, must be something to you!</u>*
>
> <u>*The Satanic Jews that control everything and mostly everybody, if they are your enemy, then you must… must be somebody.*</u>
>
> ***And if they have not been able to move you off your square [Audience shouts and applause in obvious approval at that moment]*** *! If they have thrown everything at you including the kitchen sink and maybe the toilet too, and you still standing strong, then evidently there is a force field around you that is able to withstand the "punktified" force of this world [Audience applause and shouts in obvious approval].*

So, with a little context, which the ADL does not seem to care for, we can easily understand that the ADL tries desperately to portray Farrakhan negatively and tries to trick the readers into believing something that didn't happen the way they claim. The crowd erupted because they realize and bear witness that Farrakhan has not been compromised despite the power of the US government and Satanic Jews (not to be confused with Righteous Jews).

---

[93] *How Strong Is Your Foundation: Can We Survive? Part 2*, The Final Call Online Store: https://finalcallstore.noi.org/product/how-strong-is-our-foundation-can-we-survive-part-2-dvd/.

Section 5 - Page 1, paragraph 5 of the ADL's report

The ADL states:

*In the series, titled The Time and What Must Be Done, Farrakhan frequently characterized <u>Jews as "Satanic"</u> and promoted a wide range of anti-Semitic conspiracy theories, **alleging Jewish control over government, finance, entertainment, and other sectors**.*

Once again, the ADL tries to make an amalgam or homogenization of Jews. In other words, they treat the Jewish community as a whole, which is very unfair to Jews. Some Jews may be criminals, but that does not mean all Jews are criminals. For instance, the <u>Purple Gang</u>[94] did not represent all Jews; so the claim of the ADL that Farrakhan makes that amalgam is deceptive and an outright lie.

The (so-called) Jewish Purple Gang

Image from Wikipedia

The Nation of Islam's Research Group gracefully <u>gives us access</u>[95] to evidence of the influence and mastery by the Jewish people in different spheres such as banking, Media, Radio, TV, and so on. Indeed, in *The Time And What Must Be Done* <u>Part 20</u>[96] of May 25, 2013, Farrakhan mentions starting at the 29 minute mark:

---

[94] *The Purple Gang*, Wikipedia: https://en.wikipedia.org/wiki/The_Purple_Gang.

[95] See Part 20 – (The Time & What Must Be Done): https://www.noi.org/docs/.

Jewish influence over the affairs of the world are undeniably powerful. Far out of proportion to their numbers. Their role in shaping public opinion through their Media interests and their mastery of the world of business and trade is pivotal to the world of economy. As a group, they are the most successful in terms of income and wealth and they have reached the highest echelon or the pinnacle of power in every field of human endeavor.

We have lists of Jewish influence with the Media, Jewish influence in banking, Jewish influence in government, Jewish influence in Hollywood. *We will post some of these lists for you to check on www.noi.org where this broadcast can be found. Why don't you check behind us like we're checking behind them? We are… these, hum, things are not secret. They're on the Internet. We just went and looked it up.*

Now we're posting it for you to read so that you can see we are not lying. ***They are the most powerful group and <u>unfortunately the Synagogue of Satan is leading America and this world to ruin, to destruction, to desolation</u>. These lists, we believe, prove that Jews are the masters of Hollywood. They are the masters of all forms of Media, radio, television. They are the masters of trade and commerce, banking, medicine, and law.***

Control of the government

The control of the government by so-called Jews has already been visited previously. So, let us move on.

Control of finance

Who was the Chair of the Federal Reserve in 2013 when the *Time And What Must Be Done* series was broadcasting? It was Jewish economist Ben Bernanke from 2006 to 2014. Who was Chair before him? It was Jewish economist Alan Greenspan from 1987 to 2006. Who came after Bernanke? It was Jewish economist Janet Yellen from 2014 to 2018.

---

[96] *The Time And What Must Be Done Pt 20*, The Final Call Online Store: https://finalcallstore.noi.org/product/the-time-and-what-must-be-done-pt-20-dvd/.

Ben Bernanke

Image from Wikipedia

Alan Greenspan

Image from Wikipedia

What is the Federal Reserve? According to the United States of Appeals, Eight Circuit, in the case Kennedy C. Scott v. Federal Reserve Bank of Kansas City[97], quotes the Supreme Court that:

> *Instrumentalities like the national banks or the federal reserve banks, in which there are private interests, are not departments of the government.* ***They are private corporations in which the government has an interest.***

---

[97] *SCOTT v. FEDERAL RESERVE BANK OF KANSAS CITY*, Find Law For Legal Professionals: https://caselaw.findlaw.com/us-8th-circuit/1208321.html.

If we look at the purpose of that private corporation born from the Federal Reserve Act and coming from their own website[98], we learn that:

> *The Federal Reserve Act of 1913* **established the Federal Reserve System as the central bank of the United States to provide the nation with a safer, more flexible, and more stable monetary and financial system**. *The law sets out the purposes, structure, and functions of the System as well as outlines aspects of its operations and accountability. Congress has the power to amend the Federal Reserve Act, which it has done several times over the years. The complete act, as amended, is provided here by section.*

The US debt went from 1913 to 2013 of about 3 billion dollars[99] to 17.3 trillion dollars[100]. Furthermore, the buying power of the US dollar has been reduced by 2 253%. This means that for a product worth $100 in 1913, would have cost you $2,353.10 in 2013. So apparently, the Federal Reserve did not quite accomplish its purpose. Certainly, there are many factors to explain the debt and loss of value of the US dollar, one factor was the end of gold being the standard, but the point being made here is that Jews were in control of the finance of the US through the Federal Reserve since 1987 up until 2013 when the Nation of Islam aired the series *The Time And What Must Be Done*. So, it is a fact and not "anti-Semitism".

Control of entertainment and other sectors

We have already touched the subject of the prominence of Jews in entertainment, so let us see some of the "other sectors".

Can we say "Jews" control the following sectors? We can at least certainly say that they are prominent.

---

[98] *Federal Reserve Act*, Board of Governors of the Federal Reserve System: https://www.federalreserve.gov/aboutthefed/fract.htm.

[99] *Historical Debt Outstanding – Annual 1900 – 1949*, Treasury Direct. Around 3 billion of debt in 1913: https://www.treasurydirect.gov/govt/reports/pd/histdebt/histdebt_histo3.htm.

[100] *Monthly Statement of the Public Debt of the United States*, Treasury Direct, December 31, 2013. Around 17,3 billion of debt in 2013: https://www.treasurydirect.gov/govt/reports/pd/mspd/2013/opds122013.pdf.

Alcohol:

As seen in Joel Haber's article from the Jewish Telegraphic Agency:

This may be surprising, but Jews have a long and very influential history in the alcohol industry spanning Europe, Israel and North America.[101]

and

Arnold Rothstein was recognized as "the pioneer big businessman of organized crime in the United States" as reported on the Jewish Virtual Library.[102]

Tobacco:

At Amsterdam, the first important tobacco importing and processing center in the 17th century, Isak ltaliaander was the largest importer, and 10 of the 30 leading tobacco importers were Jews.[103]

Sex trafficking:

The definition of sex trafficking found in the Victim of Trafficking and Violence Protection Act (VTVPA) of 2000 is at section 102[104]:

*(9) Trafficking includes all the elements of the crime of forcible rape when it involves the involuntary participation of another person **in sex acts** by means of **fraud**, force, or **coercion**.*

---

[101] Joel Haber, *The forgotten history of Jews in the alcohol industry,* Jewish Telegraphic Agency, July 8, 2020: https://www.jta.org/2020/07/08/food/the-forgotten-history-of-jews-in-the-alcohol-industry.

[102] *Arnold Rothstein (1882 – 1928),* Jewish Virtual Library: Arnold Rothstein (jewishvirtuallibrary.org).

[103] *Tobacco Trade And Industries,* Encyclopedia: https://www.encyclopedia.com/religion/encyclopedias-almanacs-transcripts-and-maps/tobacco-trade-and-industries.

[104] *Victims of trafficking and violence protection act of 2000,* GovInfo, October 28, 2000: https://www.govinfo.gov/content/pkg/PLAW-106publ386/pdf/PLAW-106publ386.pdf.

The definitions of "fraud" by the online Merriam-Webster:

> *Fraud: 1 a.: Deceit, **trickery**. Specifically: **intentional perversion of truth** in order to induce another **to part with something of value** or to surrender a legal right*

The definition of "**coercion**" and "commercial **sex act**" as stated in the VTVPA:

> *(2) **COERCION**.—The term ''coercion'' means—*
> *(A) threats of serious harm to or physical*
> *restraint against any person;*
> *(B) any scheme, plan, or pattern intended to cause a person to*
> *believe that failure to perform an act would result in serious*
> *harm to or physical restraint against any person; or*
> *(C) the abuse or threatened abuse of the legal process.*
>
> *(3) **COMMERCIAL SEX ACT.**—The term ''commercial sex act'' means any sex act on account of which anything of value is given to or received by any person.*

But let us at least prove that sex trafficking does exist in the (so-called) Jewish community.

Well, a recent famous case would be the so-called Jew Jeffrey Epstein, but that is too easy, isn't it?

So, what about the Bronfman sisters (Clare and Sara) with the NXIVM sex trafficking cult? See the article[105] from the Globe and Mail:

> *Two daughters of Canadian billionaire Edgar Bronfman Sr. have been accused in a New York lawsuit of **funnelling millions of dollars to a sex cult** to finance efforts to dig up dirt on opponents of the organization, including federal judges.*

---

[105] Ian Baily, *Bronfman heiresses accused of crucial financing of sex cult NXIVM in lawsuit*, The Globe and Mail, February 12, 2020: https://www.theglobeandmail.com/canada/british-columbia/article-sara-clare-bronfman-named-in-us-lawsuit-against-sex-cult-nxivm/.

Clare and Sara Bronfman

Image from Wikipedia

You might say that these are aberrations of modern time, but then comes in writer and former professor Dr. Eric Kline Silverman who published an article[106] in the Jewish Boston in May 2019 confirming that sex trafficking is (also) a Jewish issue. He states:

Sex trafficking was not uncommon among Jewish immigrants *in the Lower East Side of New York in the 1880s.*

Now let us push the envelope, but not really, and go into Hollywood and pornography as being a part of sex trafficking.

Famous case, yet underwhelming Media coverage, is Harvey Weinstein and the "couch audition[107]".

But is Harvey Weinstein's criminal behavior something new to Hollywood? Not at all.

---

[106] Eric Silverman, *Sex Trafficking Is a Jewish Issue*, Jewish Boston, May 22, 2019: https://www.jewishboston.com/sex-trafficking-is-a-jewish-issue/.

[107] Patricia Hurtado, *Weinstein Prosecutors Build Case That Casting Couch Was Trap*, Bloomberg, January 29, 2020: https://www.bloomberg.com/news/articles/2020-01-29/weinstein-casting-couch-could-save-him-or-send-him-to-prison.

Harvey Weinstein

Image from Wikipedia

Co-founder of MGM studios, Louis B. Mayer[108] (real name Lazar Meir, a so-called Jew) is known to be one of many people in the industry to have abused his position of authority to have sex with actresses. There is no doubt that if he would have lived during the Me Too movement, he would have been accused of rape and sex trafficking the same way Harvey Weinstein is right now.

First, Louis B. Mayer's "couch audition" explained here[109]. It states:

*"The perils for women in Hollywood are embedded, like land mines, from an actress's debut to her swan song," says film critic and historian Carrie Rickey, "**where moguls** like Harry Cohn **reputedly wouldn't cast starlets like Marilyn Monroe and Kim Novak unless they auditioned in bed**."*

*Long before Weinstein there was **Louis B. Mayer**, who co-founded Metro-Goldwyn-Mayer studios in 1924. **Mayer, the***

---

[108] *Louis B. Mayer*, Wikipedia: https://en.wikipedia.org/wiki/Louis_B._Mayer.

[109] Thelma Adams, *Casting-Couch Tactics Plagued Hollywood Long Before Harvey Weinstein*, Variety, October 17, 2017: https://variety.com/2017/film/features/casting-couch-hollywood-sexual-harassment-harvey-weinstein-1202589895/.

*ground zero of this kind of abuse, had means, motive, opportunity, and that critical piece of the puzzle: the whip. **If women didn't comply, he'd threaten to ruin their careers or those of their loved ones**. Sound familiar?*

Well, it certainly does sound familiar with Harvey Weinstein. In this article[110], it states:

*Several Weinstein accusers have accused Weinstein of violating the federal sex trafficking statute, **by effectively offering to exchange movie roles for sex**.*

Louis B. Mayer (1884-1957)

Image from Wikipedia

Notice also that the sex trafficking claim on him (Weinstein) still stands as mentioned in the article:

***But several judges have now allowed the claim to proceed, finding that the plaintiffs have plausibly alleged that Weinstein was engaged in "commercial sex acts."** Judge Robert W. Sweet, who died in March, wrote a ruling in August 2018 in which he held that a meeting with Weinstein could be considered a "thing of value" under the statute.*

---

[110] Gene Maddaus, *Harvey Weinstein Loses Bid to Toss Sex Trafficking Claim*, Variety, December 19, 2019: https://variety.com/2019/biz/news/harvey-weinstein-sex-trafficking-count-1203449388/.

But what about pornography?

Let us consider [this][111] as the basis by which Professor Nathan Abrams mentioned previously:

> (…) *but there's no getting away from* **the fact that secular Jews have played (and still continue to play) a disproportionate role throughout the adult film industry in America**.
> (…)
> **Though Jews make up only two per cent of the American population, they have been prominent in pornography**. <u>*Many erotica dealers in the book trade*</u> *between 1890 and 1940* <u>*were immigrant Jews*</u> *of German origin.*

Professor Nathan Abrams

Image from Wikipedia

So, not only did those so-called Jews bring their filth from Germany, but they also thrived in it once they arrived in the USA; Reuben Sturman the "Walt Disney of Porn"; Steven Hirsch the "Donald Trump of porno"?

---

[111] Nathan Abrams, *Nathan Abrams On Jews in The American Porn Industry*, SCRIBD, 2004: https://fr.scribd.com/document/135073670/Nathan-Abrams-on-Jews-in-the-American-Porn-Industry.

What about this that Professor Abrams mentions:

> ***Jews accounted for most of the leading male performers*** *as well as a sizeable number of female stars in porn movies of the 1970s and '80s. The doyen of the Hebrew studs is Ron Jeremy.*

So now that the involvement in pornography by (so-called) Jews is well established, let us get to the part about "sex trafficking".

Remember the definitions about "**fraud**", "**coercing**" and "commercial **sex act**" which are prerequisites of the definition of "**sex trafficking**" by the VTVPA? Here is where I use them.

Wouldn't you agree that pornographic actresses receive something of value (money) for a sex act? The answer is probably yes. <u>We are not asking if pornography is legal or not</u>. That is irrelevant because slavery was openly legal for 310 years and it still is with the 13th Amendment, but it does not make it right and in accordance with the spirit of the Torah, the Gospel and the Holy Qur'an.

Wouldn't you agree that young women are tricked into pornography? Well, here[112] is a fresh example of such from San Diego:

> *In the civil lawsuit, the women said that they* ***had applied for modeling jobs*** *and later flown to San Diego from their hometowns.*

> *They were put up in hotel rooms* ***before being told they would be making sex videos****, for which they were paid $5,000.*

Notice the name of one of the co-owners of the website: Matthew **Isaac Wolfe**.

---

[112] Karen Ruiz, *At least 100 more women claim they are victims of GirlsDoPorn site that forced them to star in sex films that were posted online without their consent*, Daily Mail, January 7, 2020: https://www.dailymail.co.uk/news/article-7858901/At-100-women-come-forward-claims-against-GirlsDoPorn-scheme.html.

Here[113] is another example which was featured at the Sundance Film Festival in 2015, the documentary Hot Girls Wanted:

> *When Rachel Bernard from Oswego, Illinois, answered a Craigslist ad last fall entitled "Hot Girls Wanted"* **that promised a modeling gig and a free trip to Miami**, *she thought it might be her ticket to freedom and fame.*
> *(…)*
> *"They emailed me back, telling me that* **it was actually adult entertainment,** *and you can get $2,000-$3,000 for going out there once," she said.*

About the coercive part of the matter, professional pornographic actresses have contracts. What are the chances that if they decide to not "perform" or if they complain, they will be sued? You might say it is a hypothetical question which does not deserve an answer. But it is a relevant question. Matter of fact, here[114] is an example:

> *Benz claimed when she was asked during the exit interview if she would work with Tony T. again,* **she said the director forced her to say "yes" or she would not be paid**.

To conclude on this topic (sex trafficking), let us see what Ph D Catharine Alice MacKinnon mentioned[115] in the Michigan Journal of International Law, volume 26 issue 4, 2005:

> *In material reality,* **pornography is one way women and children are trafficked for sex**. *To make visual pornography, the bulk of the industry's products, real* **women and children, and some men, are rented out for use in commercial sex acts**. *In the*

---

[113] Rebecca Jarvis, Nikki Battiste and Teri Whitcraft, *'Hot Girls Wanted': How Teen Girls Seeking Fame Can Be Lured into Amateur Porn*, ABC News, June 4, 2015: https://abcnews.go.com/US/hot-girls-wanted-teen-girls-seeking-fame-lured/story?id=31290984.

[114] Kathleen Joyce, *Porn star sues company, director and performer for alleged sexual battery*, New York Post, April 10, 2018: https://nypost.com/2018/04/10/porn-star-sues-company-director-and-performer-for-alleged-sexual-battery/.

[115] Catharine A. MacKinnon, *Pornography as Trafficking*, Michigan Journal of International Law, Volume 26, Issue 4, 2005: https://repository.law.umich.edu/cgi/viewcontent.cgi?article=1241&context=mjil.

*resulting materials, these people are then conveyed and sold for a
buyer's sexual use.*

So, considering what Professor Nathan Abrams mentioned: "**the fact
that secular Jews have played (and still continue to play) a
disproportionate role throughout he adult film industry in
America**", we can say that (so-called) Jews are quite prominent in
sex trafficking.

The ADL states that:

> *In March 2013, Farrakhan spoke at Tuskegee University*[116] *where he told college and high school students that* **President Barack Obama was "selected" by whites to do their bidding before he was elected by the people** *and that* **the U.S. government brings cancer and other illnesses into Black communities as part of a larger policy of depopulation.** *During a sermon at Fellowship Chapel in Detroit in May 2013*[117]*, Farrakhan told the audience that* **the "Synagogue of Satan," a phrase he uses repeatedly to refer to Jews,** *has* **"mastered civilization now, but they've mastered it in evil,"** *using its control of Hollywood and the media to* **"put you before the world in this disgraceful matter."**

Let us break this down into two parts: The March lecture and the May lecture.

March 2013 Tuskegee University lecture

First of all, look how arrogant the ADL is to demand the president of Tuskegee University, Dr. Gilbert L. Rochon, to repudiate[118] Farrakhan:

> **The Anti-Defamation League today sent a letter to Tuskegee University president Dr. Gilbert L. Rochon urging that he repudiate** *the anti-Semitic and anti-white rhetoric of* **Nation of Islam leader Louis Farrakhan** *in advance of Minister Farrakhan's speech at Tuskegee next week.*

---

[116] *Tuskegee University: The Seminal Fluid Of The Kingdom Of God*, The Final Call Online Store, March 22, 2013: https://finalcallstore.noi.org/product/tuskegee-university-the-seminal-fluid-of-the-kingdom-of-god-dvd/.

[117] *The Time And What Must Be Done, Detroit*, The Final Call Online Store, May 17, 2013. At the Fellowship Chapel, Detroit, Michigan: https://finalcallstore.noi.org/product/the-time-and-what-must-be-done-detroit-dvd/.

[118] *ADL Urges Tuskegee University President: Repudiate Hate Speech of Louis Farrakhan Before Campus Visit*, ADL, March 14, 2013: https://atlanta.adl.org/adl-urges-tuskegee-university-president-repudiate-hate-speech-of-louis-farrakhan-before-campus-visit/.

About President Obama, here is what Farrakhan actually said as heard in the CD[119] starting at 37 minutes 43 seconds:

> *But the crab master picks some of us out. You didn't hear me. "You know, I'm the first to have dinner with the governor." "I'm the first to be this." "I'm the first to be that." See, he picked you out. Did you know that Barack Obama was selected before he was elected? Who selected him? For what purpose? We thought: "Wow! This is beautiful. Our brother! I never thought I would live to see a Black man in the White House." White folks will put you there to deceive the rest. Making you think that you've got a home now.*
>
> *So, you're waving your flags. Never was there a president before him that you went and started waving flags. You understood that the American flag was like the Confederate flag because you caught hell under both those flags. Otherwise! The Tuskegee airmen that wanted to fight for America, they had to fly in old planes until they proved they could save white people in bombers.*

As you can see, he did not mention "to do their bidding before he was elected by the people". The ADL's writers apparently let their subconscious slip there; basically, telling what actually happened to Barack Obama.

In any case, the "selected before elected" part is a matter of fact. To become the presidential nominee, one has to be selected by the party one is in. Here[120], on Wikipedia, the results of the 2008 Democratic Party presidential primaries are shown. A look at Obama's two term cabinet[121] does not indicate favoritism for Blacks or so-called minorities. A look at his 2008[122] or 2012[123] top donors show that

---

[119] See note 116.

[120] *Results of the 2008 Democratic Party presidential primaries*, Wikipedia: https://en.wikipedia.org/wiki/Results_of_the_2008_Democratic_Party_presidential_primaries.

[121] *Confirmations of Barack Obama's Cabinet*, Wikipedia: https://en.wikipedia.org/wiki/Confirmations_of_Barack_Obama%27s_Cabinet.

[122] Andrew Clark, *Bankers and academics at top of donor list*, The Guardian, November 8, 2008: https://www.theguardian.com/world/2008/nov/08/barackobama-wallstreet-bankers-campaign-donations-goldmansachs.

white people and white businesses[124] had big interest in him. Of course, they have the right to help a candidate they feel will benefit them. That is natural.

About the policy of depopulation of the U.S. government, here is what Farrakhan says about it in this excerpt[125] of the whole lecture.

Now here in 1974 **Henry Kissinger***… Have you heard of him? (Crowd answers yes)… who was then Secretary of State under President Nixon signed* **National Security Memorandum 200** *titled… listen to the tile…* **"Implications of worldwide population growth for U.S. security and overseas interests."** *And that memorandum 200 was signed and adopted as official policy of the government of the United States in 1975 by President Gerald Ford. Now what is this policy? Listen to the words in the memorandum. Now what I'm saying you can research it yourself. Listen to the words.*

> **Depopulation should be the highest priority of U.S. foreign policy towards the Third World.**

He quoted reasons of national security:

> *And because the U.S. economy will require large and increasing amounts of minerals from abroad, especially from less developed countries.* **Wherever a lessening of population can increase the prospects for such stability, population policy becomes relevant to resources supplies and to the economic interest of the United States.**

Depopulation is now policy of our government.

---

[123] Associated Press, *Who are top 5 donors to Obama, Romney campaigns?*, Politico, October 19, 2012: https://www.politico.com/story/2012/10/who-are-top-5-donors-to-obama-romney-campaigns-082637.

[124] *Top Contributors, 2008 Cycle*, OpenSecrets: https://www.opensecrets.org/pres08/contrib.php?cid=n00009638.

[125] *Farrakhan @ Tuskegee University, Exposing The U.S. Government on Campus*, YouTube, March 22, 2013: https://www.youtube.com/watch?v=SM63OMZQDmI.

Isn't it interesting that Henry Kissinger (real first name Heinz) is a so-called Jew and that people from the Third World happen to be the darker people?

What Farrakhan has said about the depopulation policy of the U.S. government is absolutely true and can be read from the infamous Kissinger's report/memorandum found here[126]. On page 9 and 10, we get the picture that they want to reduce the population by 3 billion.

> *29. While specific goals in this area are difficult to state, our aim should be for the world to achieve a replacement level of fertility, (a two- child family on the average), by about the year 2000.* ***This will require the present 2 percent growth rate to decline to 1.7 percent within a decade and to 1.1 percent by 2000*** *compared to the U.N medium projection,* ***this goal would result in 500 million fewer people in 2000 and about 3 billion fewer in 2050. Attainment of this goal will require greatly intensified population programs.*** *A basis for developing national population growth control targets to achieve this world target is contained in the World Population Plan of Action.*

It does not get any clearer than this. Just to make sure you get it right; it is a **<u>GOAL</u>** to reduce the population by 3 billion people by the year 2050. The use of contraception, abortion, so-called education, and the use of mass media are a few of the tactics mentioned in that report.

May 2013 Fellowship Chapel lecture

The ADL claims:

> (…) *Farrakhan told the audience that* ***the "Synagogue of Satan," a phrase he uses repeatedly to refer to Jews*** *(…)*

---

[126] *National Security Study Memorandum NSSM 200 Implications of Worldwide Population Growth For U.S. Security and Overseas Interests (THE KISSINGER REPORT)*, December 10, 1974: https://pdf.usaid.gov/pdf_docs/PCAAB500.pdf.

Once more, the ADL injects its own interpretation and falsehood to what Farrakhan says and means. Let's make a jump in the past. Let's go to Saviours' Day 1990[127].

> *And you do with me as is written but remember that I have warned you that Allah will punish you. You are wicked deceivers of the American people. You have sucked their blood. You are not real Jews, __those of you__ that are not real Jews. **You are the Synagogue of Satan**, and you have wrapped your tentacles around the U.S. government, and you are deceiving and sending this nation to hell. But I warn you in the name of Allah, you would be wise to leave me alone. But if you choose to crucify me, know that Allah will crucify you.*

So, Farrakhan clearly breaks down the Jewish community into at least two groups here: the real Jews and the fake ones. We can also hear from the CD at the Fellowship Chapel where he discusses the transatlantic slave trade, starting at 1 hour 51 seconds:

> *Now, I'm not talking to the good Jewish people. I'm not talking to you. **Because the good Jews are those who try to live by the commandments and statutes of God.***

This goes along, as seen previously, with the clear distinction Allah/God does in the Bible and the Qur'an. So, there is nothing wrong with what he said. It only goes to show that the ADL repeatedly tries to make the Jewish community as an indivisible whole, which is laughable at its face value. ·

How so? One only needs to see how many different denominations[128], also known as movements or branches there are. The Jewish religion must understand that it is not a homogenous group at all. We have the reform Jews, the orthodox Jews, the ultra-orthodox Jews, the secular Jews and so on.

---

[127] *"When the sun rises in the west; Saviours' Day '90"*, YouTube. At Mosque Maryam in Chicago, IL. on February 25, 1990: https://www.youtube.com/watch?v=KoNPoQmhNyQ.

[128] *Jewish religious movements*, Wikipedia: https://en.wikipedia.org/wiki/Jewish_religious_movements.

No matter how many denominations there could be, the right thing to do is to split any group into two groups: those who believe and practice the teachings of the prophet(s) they claim to follow, and those who do lip service.

So, let us go back to the sermon at Fellowship Chapel in Detroit. The ADL claims that:

> (...) (Synagogue of Satan) "has mastered civilization now, but they've mastered it in evil," using its control of Hollywood and the media to "put you before the world in this disgraceful matter."

Let us give a little context to it, although it is 100% true that the Synagogue of Satan uses its control of Hollywood. Farrakhan, after mentioning he went to an Eddie Murphy show and speaking about the reaction of the crowd, says to the audience, starting at 1 hour 9 minutes 13 seconds:

> I said: "What is going on here?" See, now, you turn on your TV, they're feeding you filth. The comedians feeding you filth and you sucking it up.
>
> Now they have these, what do they call them? Reality shows! And what is your reality that you could be found wasting time in front of foolishness.
>
> **And the Enemy that owns that**, it's the same people that own Hollywood. The same people that control your press. The same people that control your media. The same people who are the publishers. The same people who are the distributors. **The SAME Synagogue of Satan!** <u>**And they put you before the world in this disgraceful manner**</u>. Who owns the record companies that we could go and call our women out of their name and glorify the worst of ghetto life?

Let us touch a little bit about the exploitation of Black artists since we've already established the prominent role of the so-called Jews in the entertainment industry as we have seen in Sections 2 and 5 of this analysis. It will further back up what is quoted in the previous paragraph.

Let us introduce PhD (Dr.) Wesley Muhammad, scholar, student minister and part of the Research Group of the Nation of Islam.

Ph D (Dr.) Wesley Muhammad

Image from the Final Call Newspapers[129]

Among many books he wrote, I must refer you to his 2020 book: Understanding the assault on the Black man Vol. 2 - The Pot Plot[130]. In that book that I have quickly skimmed through and have yet to read completely, he has a section about Hip Hop.

Image from DrWesley.online

---

[129] Ebony Safiyyah Muhammad, *LGBTQ opposition to Dr. Wesley Muhammad rises*, The Final Call, December 6, 2017:
https://www.finalcall.com/artman/publish/National_News_2/article_103909.shtml.

[130] You can buy the book at Dr. Wesley Muhammad's website:
https://www.drwesley.online/publications.

In it, and I must insist that almost every single page has footnotes for his sources, we learn, along with many other things, **of the disproportionate presence of (so-called) Jews in key positions to influence a type of music (Hip-Hop) that has nothing to do with Jewish culture when it (Hip Hop) was created**.

Page 580 has a diagram of "The Architecture of "Illuminati" influence on Hip Hop". Evidently, we can replace "Illuminati" by (so-called) "Jews". Indeed, at the top of that architecture are Len Blavatnik, Edgar Bronfman, David Geffen and Sumner Redstone (Rothstein).

Is it normal that Lyor Cohen (referred as an Israeli American on Wikipedia's previously mentioned list[131]) was at the head of 300 Entertainment and was a former president of Def Jam Recordings? These labels employ (rather own to be more precise) several Hip-Hop artists. Mr. Cohen is linked with Edgar Bronfman's investor group.

Lyor Cohen

Image from Wikipedia

Is it normal that the Late Sumner Murray Rothstein was the owner of Black Entertainment Television (BET)?

---

131 See note 37.

These are just 2 examples of well-established companies whom the masses would be tricked into thinking they belong to Black entrepreneurs or that the product sold comes from a Black mind.

These so-called Jews certainly pervert and put the Black artists before the world in disgraceful manner. One only has to think about Cardi B and Megan Thee Stallion's video "WAP" (Wet Ass Pussy) to understand the disgraceful image put forward by the Synagogue of Satan.

Megan Thee Stallion (left) and Cardi B (right)

Image from Wikipedia

The definition of the verb to pervert, by the online Merriam-Webster dictionary[132]:

> *1 a.: to cause to turn aside or away from what is good or true or morally right: corrupt.'*

Have the so-called Jews turned away Black entertainers and athletes from what is morally right? Yes.

---

[132] From the Merriam-Webster online dictionary: https://www.merriam-webster.com/dictionary/pervert.

We have already established the prominence of Talmudic Jews in the entertainment.

Let us look at Scriptures from the Torah. Here is what Deuteronomy chapter 22, verse 5 (KJV) tells us:

> *The woman shall not wear that which pertaineth unto a man,* ***neither shall a man put on a woman's garment: for all that do so are*** **_abomination_** ***unto the LORD thy God***.

Are Black actors being tricked into wearing dresses in Hollywood? Yes, they are. Here is a list[133], from the article *Emasculating The Black Male: 15 Actors Who Wore a Dress For Success,* of those who have done it and have had successful careers: Eddie Murphy, Jamie Foxx, Chris Tucker, Wesley Snipes, Martin Lawrence, Brandon T. Jackson, Tyler Perry, Arsenio Hall, Flip Wilson, Miguel Nunez Jr., Kenan Thomas, Ving Rhames, Tracy Morgan, Marlon Wayans, Shawn Wayans. These are just a few.

We can especially appreciate that the article starts with Dave Chappelle's complaint on the Oprah Show. Oprah's facial expression (close friend of Harvey Weinstein by the way), as Chappelle exposes the trick used by Hollywood to put Blacks into dresses, is very relevant. As if she is thinking, but it's only my opinion: "you're not supposed to speak about it. You are going to get me into trouble."

Dave Chappelle talks about the movie Blue Streak in which he had a role with Martin Lawrence (who wore many dresses in his career) and how he was pressured by the writers, the producer, and the director into putting a dress; but he refused.

He says:

> *Guy[134]* ***comes back ten minutes later with a whole new scene!*** *How the hell did you write the scene so fast?*

---

[133] Leo, *Emasculating The Black Male: 15 Actors Who Wore a Dress For Success*, Atlanta Black Star, November 5, 2013: https://atlantablackstar.com/2013/11/05/emasculating-the-black-male-15-actors-who-wore-a-dress-for-success/.

[134] "Guy" is probably the writer.

Dave Chappelle's admirable steadfast stance confirms what is written in James, chapter 4, verse 7:

> *Submit yourselves therefore to God.* **Resist the devil, and he will flee from you**.

The writer, John Blumenthal[135], and the producers, Toby Jaffe and Neal H. Moritz[136], are (so-called) Jewish. This is very revealing about Hollywood Jews wanting to emasculate Black actors. Just like Satan, they suggested an abomination to a direct descendant of the Originator.

Wouldn't you qualify it as an attempt to pervert a Black male?

Look how Pharrell Williams is a bit lost in his "spiritual warfare" he mentions in this interview:

https://www.gq.com/story/pharrell-new-masculinity-cover-interview[137].

Image from gq.com

---

[135] *John Blumenthal*, Wikipedia: https://en.wikipedia.org/wiki/John_Blumenthal.

[136] *Neal H. Moritz*, Wikipedia: https://en.wikipedia.org/wiki/Neal_H._Moritz.

[137] Will Welch, *Pharrell on Evolving Masculinity and "Spiritual Warfare"*, GQ, October 14, 2019: https://www.gq.com/story/pharrell-new-masculinity-cover-interview.

Let us keep in mind that this is to expose the disgraceful way Black people, such as Pharrell Williams, are shown to the world, and not an attempt to put down the victims (like him) of such wicked minds of the Synagogue of Satan.

> ***Pharrell W.: I'll bring God into it***. *A lot of people pray less. So now when you ask a question, where do you get your number one result? Google. You don't [makes prayer hands], you [makes typing motion].*
> *(…)*

> *That's right. And what did you just say? Followers. We're followers.* ***And we're not following God. We're following men. So that's spiritual warfare.***
> *(…)*

> ***The Interviewer:*** *The musicians who are following in your footsteps* **when it comes to blurring the gender lines of fashion—the Young Thugs and Lil Uzis—they're into that.** *That's totally for them.*

> ***Pharrell W.:*** *And my point is, why not? What rule [is there]?* ***And when people start using religion as the reason someone shouldn't wear something,*** *I'm like, what are you talking about?* ***There was no such thing as a bra or blouse in any of the old sacred texts.***

So evidently, Pharrell Williams is not aware of Deuteronomy, chapter 22, verse 5.

As 1 Corinthians chapter 13, verse 33 states:

> *For God is not the author of confusion, but of peace, as in all churches of the saints.*

And a reminder that Malachi, chapter 3, verse 6, states:

> ***For I am the Lord, I change not;*** *therefore, ye sons of Jacob are not consumed.*

Furthermore, he claims wanting to bring God in the issue, but when religion invites itself in the discussion, then it is not welcomed. The point is not to put him down for that. It is proving he is confused. His confusion, because of his status as a celebrity, can have his "followers" or fans go astray into something declared as an abomination.

But why is it an abomination to cross-dress, acting or surgically trying to be like the opposite sex? I refer you to the wonderful book called "7 Speeches by Minister Louis Farrakhan National Representative of The Honorable Elijah Muhammad[138]" page 150. It is an interview and a relevant part to bring up to explain why it is an abomination (hateful) is this one:

> **Question:** *Does that mean God is not a woman?*
>
> **Answer:** *Well, since The Honorable Elijah Muhammad teaches us that **God created man and He also created woman, woman is as much a part of God as man**. So, when you say man is God you cannot negate woman. Woman is a part of man and man cannot come into existence or man cannot procreate, or further himself, except through a woman. And so, The Honorable Elijah Muhammad, in his Teaching, **lifts the woman into a position of great respect for it is through the woman that the nation is born**. So, any man who disrespects his woman, any man who does not protect his woman, any man who does not maintain his woman is a man who cannot maintain and respect himself.*

---

[138] Minister Louis Farrakhan, *Seven Speeches*, The Final Call Online Store: https://finalcallstore.noi.org/product/seven-speeches/.

Image from Amazon

One cannot disrespect the divinity of Woman by trying to be and/or look like one. The same goes for the divinity of Man. You do not go around trying to imitate a creature that you are not and who was fashioned in <u>the image</u> of Allah. God is not mocked (Galatians 6:7).

But then, a wicked person could try to twist Allah's word when bringing Proverbs chapter 27, verse 7:

> **For as he thinketh in his heart, so is he**: *Eat and drink, saith he to thee; but his heart is not with thee.*

The verse preceding that one is:

> *Eat thou not <u>the bread of him that hath an evil eye</u>, neither desire thou his dainty meats*

God is referring to one's nature (evil or righteous) and not at someone's gender identity. That is the kind of twisting that some people use to justify their sins such as eating swine because of Matthew chapter 15, verse 11:

> *Not that which goeth into the mouth defileth a man; but that which cometh out of the mouth, this defileth a man.*

Let us go back to Hip-Hop. In Dr. Wesley Muhammad's book, he refers to the following excerpt of an interview[139] in which Hip-Hop artist Too Short describes **how he saw conscious Hip-Hop being replaced by the filth we see since the 1990s**. He even names the (so-called) Jew who turned him from what is morally right, Barry Weiss.

> (…) *I would talk to people at **Jive** [Records], I would go talk to the **President, Barry Weiss**, and he was like…*
> (…)
> *I had made a verbal deal with **Barry Weiss, where he was like**, "Right now would be the perfect time, you should do like the raunchiest Too Short album ever – the album cover, the songs, **just do a dirty fuckin' Too Short album**." **This is the executive running the company advising me to put out an entire album of just cursing and sex**.*
> (…)
> *I started noticing at that time in Hip Hop that the **labels were actually signing the artists and promoting the artists who would bring in just the negative messages**: **let's have sex, drop ya booty**. We getting off into Crunk now, the bling bling is out there …*

Todd Anthony Shaw (Too Short)

Image from Wikipedia

---

[139] Paul Arnold, *TOO SHORT SAYS THERE WAS AN INDUSTRY-WIDE PLOT TO SHUT DOWN CONSCIOUS HIP HOP*, HipHopDX, February 29, 2012: https://hiphopdx.com/news/id.18861/title.too-short-says-there-was-an-industry-wide-plot-to-shut-down-conscious-hip-hop#.

Wouldn't you agree that what happened in Hip Hop in the 1990s is qualifying as "to pervert"? And does it have implication on the youth? We can add to the discussion the obvious promotion of drugs (pot, ecstasy) in Hip-Hop. Dr. Muhammad's book is highly recommended to the reader.

This article[140] about the influence of Hip-Hop on the youth asserts that it does have a negative effect. It even explains how it happened:

> *"What's changed over time is the greater sexualization of hip-hop. Initially, it started off as a revolutionary form of music. Now,* **large corporations produce images that sell, and there is a blatant link between hip-hop and pornography***," Dr. West said.*

Isn't it an extraordinary coincidence that both industries are prominent by (so-called) Jews?

It is not a coincidence, and it proves what Farrakhan said in his lecture at the Fellowship Chapel.

---

[140] Kathy Saengian, *Researcher cites negative influences of hip-hop*, Pittsburgh Post-Gazette, June 13, 2008: https://www.post-gazette.com/life/lifestyle/2008/06/13/Researcher-cites-negative-influences-of-hip-hop/stories/200806130124.

The ADL claims that:

*(...), Farrakhan has heavily promoted <u>the second volume</u>[141] of the NOI's anti-Semitic book <u>**The Secret Relationship Between Blacks and Jews**</u>[142]. This volume, subtitled, "How Jews Gained Control of the Black American Economy," <u>blames Jews for promoting a myth of black racial inferiority</u> and <u>makes a range of conspiratorial accusations about Jewish involvement in the slave trade and in the cotton, textiles, and banking industries.</u> Both books, according to Farrakhan, should be taught in schools across the U.S.*

This volume (...) blames Jews for promoting a myth of black racial inferiority

Well, there is no myth as seen in Section 2 of this analysis. Read the sub-section: *Jewish people were responsible for the slave trade.* The Talmud is very clear about the inferiority of Blacks as also reported by Dr. Harold Brackman. Volume 2 of the 3-part series quotes Dr. Brackman (among many other Jewish scholars) in 16 different places confirming the involvement in the slave trade.

Let us quote a passage from the book which quotes *The Jew accused*[143] by Lindemann. Page 84 of the book:

(...) in 1896 the editors of the Jewish South newspaper opined, "Negroes are intellectually, morally, and physically an inferior race – a fact none can deny."

---

[141] Nation of Islam Historical Research Department, *The Secret Relationship Between Blacks and Jews Volume 2*, The Final Call Online Store: https://finalcallstore.noi.org/product/the-secret-relationship-between-blacks-and-jews-volume-2/.

[142] Nation of Islam Historical Research Department, *The Secret Relationship Between Blacks and Jews Volume 1*, The Final Call Online Store: https://finalcallstore.noi.org/product/the-secret-relationship-between-blacks-and-jews-volume-1/.

[143] Albert S. Lindemann, *The Jew Accused Three Anti-Semitic Affairs Dreyfus, Beilis, Frank, 1894-1915*, Google Books. See page 194: https://books.google.ca/books?id=YCugGyqkYBQC&printsec=frontcover&dq=the+jew+accused+books&hl=en&sa=X&ved=2ahUKEwidnqHYmb3sAhVDgnIEHQZsDwwQ6AEwAHoECAIQAg#v=onepage&q=the%20jew%20accused%20books&f=false.

Well, well, well…

Let us add to this from the same newspaper (the Jewish South) the
"Jewish Sentiment[144]" about Black people in the army as written by
Herbert T. Ezekiel, on the June 24, 1898 issue, quoting the Hebrew
Globe Newspaper from the North:

> *Jewish Sentiment says* **it is unfortunate that negroes should be
> accepted in the United States Army except as servants**. *This is
> true in one sense,* **for they are ignorant and unruly set**. *But then
> they are equally as efficient as the white men when it comes to
> stopping bullets.* **And they make fine looking corpses**. *– Hebrew
> Globe, Syracuse, N. Y.*

> JEWISH *Sentiment* says it is unfortunate that ne-
> groes should be accepted in the United States Army
> except as servants. This is true in one sense, for they
> are an ignorant and unruly set. But then they are
> equally as efficient as the white men when it comes to
> stopping bullets. And they make fine looking
> corpses.—*Hebrew Globe, Syracuse, N. Y.*

Image from newspapers.com

So not only do the Jews see themselves as distinct of the white race,
but the Hebrew Globe seems to devalue even more the Black
people's life. In another issue[145], May 19, 1899, the writer mentions
the Dreyfus case in France and makes this remark while complaining
about the way the French people treat Jews as vermin:

> *This may seem strange and even monstrous in a nation which
> proclaimed the "rights of man," with the wildest enthusiasm and
> with an ostentatious contempt for all reserves and limitations,
> giving full civil equality, in form, to Jews* **as well as to negroes
> and other inferior races**, *more than a hundred years ago.*

---

[144] Herbert T. Ezekiel, The Jewish South, June 24, 1898:
https://www.newspapers.com/image/89032900/?terms=negroes.
[145] Herbert T. Ezekiel, The Jewish South, May 19, 1899:
https://www.newspapers.com/image/89033324.

> hunted down without law or mercy. This may seem
> strange and even monstrous in a nation which pro-
> claimed the "rights of man," with the wildest enthu-
> siasm and with an ostentatious contempt for all re-
> serves and limitations, giving full civil equality, in
> form, to Jews as well as to negroes and other inferior
> races, more than a hundred years ago. But recent

Image from newspapers.com

The establishment by (so-called) Jews that (so-called) negroes are part of an inferior race is quite evident and again, can be traced back to the Talmud as seen previously in this analysis.

This volume (…) makes a range of conspiratorial accusations about Jewish involvement in the slave trade and in the cotton, textiles, and banking industries

This lie, it being conspiratorial accusations, is already pretty much dealt with on Section 2 of this analysis. The involvement of the Jewish community in the transatlantic slave trade is a fact.

All three volumes about the Secret Relationship Between Blacks and Jews is recommended to the reader.

The first volume (Secret Relationship Between Blacks and Jews) states in the introduction:

*Deep within the recesses of the Jewish historical record is **the irrefutable evidence that <u>the most prominent of the Jewish pilgrim fathers</u> used kidnapped Black Africans disproportionately more than any other ethnic or religious group** in New World history and participated in every aspect of the international slave trade.*

No one has been able to refute this statement, although Dr. Harold Brackman wrote a book[146], based on a straw man fallacy he made up[147], claiming that Volume One's thesis is:

*The central thesis of volume one was **that Jewish merchants**, in fact were responsible for considerably less than two percent of the traffic of enslaved people between Africa and the Americas **"dominated" the Atlantic Slave Trade**.*

Image from Amazon

So, we can clearly see the straw man fallacy in bold. And his irrelevant and silly report is only 100 pages while the book by the

---

[146] Dr. Harold Brackman, *Ministry of Lies: The Truth Behind The Secret Relationship Between Blacks and Jews*, September 14, 1994. Sold on GoodReads: https://www.goodreads.com/book/show/438697.Ministry_of_Lies.

[147] Dr Harold Brackman's report "Louis Farrakhan – Four Decades of Bigotry in his own words, as shown on the Wiesenthal's website: http://www.wiesenthal.com/assets/pdf/new-swc-report-farrakhan.pdf?fbclid=IwAR0w4bmYjBkpMV_pApvouEqqGmqzfd2LQYNOm6Eq2d8H-Br_MHiRX5Cp-74.

This report is filled with lies, distortions and so on to defame Farrakhan. An analysis of Dr. Brackman's defamatory report for the Simon Wiesenthal Center is available at the following link. I wrote it in July 2020.
https://drive.google.com/drive/folders/1epnTmST6VqUsnNaeIJm9bhTfOzQRy1zQ?usp=sharing.

Nation of Islam is 334 pages. Does that make sense to you when we are already at page 97 in this ongoing analysis yet at page 2 of the ADL's report? Precisely!

The third volume[148] is about the Leo Frank case. A so-called Jew accused by a Black man, James Conley, of murdering a white child, Mary Phagan in 1913. Despite being in the South, despite everyone in the court case being white (jury, prosecutor, judge), they found Leo Frank guilty of murder.

Image from the Final Call Store

The ADL worked very hard to obtain a posthumous pardon[149] for the murderer of Mary Phagan.

They still work very hard to portray Leo Frank as the victim of anti-Semitism by white people[150] and claiming he was falsely accused. In other words, that the Black janitor, James Conley, lied.

---

[148] Nation of Islam Historical Research Department, *The Secret Relationship Between Blacks and Jews Volume 3*, The Final Call Online Store: https://finalcallstore.noi.org/product/the-secret-relationship-between-blacks-and-jews-volume-3/.

[149] *Remembering Leo Frank*, ADL: https://www.adl.org/resources/backgrounders/remembering-leo-frank.

[150] *ADL: Anti-Semitism Around Leo Frank Case Flourishes on 100th Anniversary*, ADL: https://www.adl.org/news/press-releases/adl-anti-semitism-around-leo-frank-case-flourishes-on-100th-anniversary.

So, we are supposed to believe that a Black man (**from the South in the most anti-Black country of the era and during the disenfranchisement, Black codes and Jim Crow laws in effect**) was responsible for the murder of a 13 years old white child and that the white citizens looked the other way of all the evidence supposedly condemning him (according to the so-called Jewish community) to lynch, with the involvement of the KKK, an innocent white Jewish business man in a State with deep Jewish roots. All that because of anti-Semitism.

Well, how do they explain that the KKK celebrated[151] in 1924 the 50th anniversary of a story of a local Jewish merchant (Emanuel Steiner) as reported in the newspaper *The Republic* in Indiana?

The Ku Klux Klan in Fairfield, Ill., called on Emanuel Steiner, Jewish clothing merchant. But it was a friendly visit. The Klansmen came to present him with a wreath of American beauty roses on the occasion of the 50th anniversary of the opening of his store. The presentation was made by the Rev. Herbert G. Markley, pastor of the Fairfield Presbyterian church, secretary of the Fairfield branch of the Klan.

Image from newspapers.com[152]

---

[151] *Klansmen present wreath to Jew*, The Evening Republican, September 2, 1924. As seen on Newspapers.com:
https://www.newspapers.com/image/?clipping_id=24913758&fcfToken=eyJhbGciOiJIUzI1NiIsInR5cCI6IkpXVCJ9.eyJmcmVlLXZpZXctaWQiOjEzMDk3MzYyOCwiaWF0IjoxNTk1NTU1Mzg3LCJleHAiOjE1OTU2NDE3ODd9.Mzk6NV2_kM3hog_ucVXaRyRjDBCav8wh6NM5iNcvyag.

[152] *Klansmen present wreath to Jew*, The Evening Republican, September 2, 1924:
https://www.newspapers.com/clip/24913758/steinerkkk/.

Conclusion

The Verdict

We have now arrived at the end of the first volume.

The reader may have noticed that the ADL has not really provided any evidence of what it claims of the Honorable Minister Louis Farrakhan. Making baseless accusations of hateful speech, bigotry, extremism, and anti-Semitism without ever backing a single claim with facts. Rather, the only things provided by the ADL are innuendos, lies, distortions, straw man fallacies and out of context half-quotes, all in the hopes that one would accept the claims at face value.

This is evidently wicked, deceptive, and aimed at manipulating the reader. Indeed, the ADL's intent is to trigger raw emotions and depict a man in a way that people would find his demise justifiable, and maybe even cheer for it. Does this situation ring a bell to the reader about a man who lived 2,000 years ago? We will get back at this in a short while.

The ADL boasts about its Jewish values shown on the website[153] claiming that they:

> *... inform our work and the change we seek in the world. These values also guide the strategy and tactics of all of our programs and activities globally, nationally and locally.*

It is worth highlighting that out of their 8 core values the numbers 1, 6, 7 and 8, as outlined below, are absent from their report:

1. We have the **courage** to speak out against antisemitism and bigotry, discrimination and injustice—even when we stand alone.
2. We always observe the highest standards of **integrity**.

---

[153] *Our Values*, ADL: https://www.adl.org/who-we-are/our-values.

3. We are viewed as having unquestioned **credibility** because our actions draw from years of experience and are grounded in research and rigorous thinking.
4. We set high performance expectations and hold ourselves **accountable** for the quality of our work and the results we achieve as individuals, as a team and as one organization.

Tell me, where is the **courage** and **credibility** if the ADL, as an institution, is not **accountable** for a report that outstandingly lacks **integrity**?

Well, if those four concepts are part of Jewish values, and they are, and we can't find any of those four in the report by the ADL, the only conclusion is that the people who participated in it are not Jews. So, who are they? Coming full circle now. Revelation chapter 2, verse 9, KJV:

> *I know thy works, and tribulation, and poverty, (but thou art rich) and I know* ***the blasphemy of them which say they are Jews, and are not, but are the Synagogue of Satan***.

The ADL's nature qualifies for verse 12 in the book of Ephesians, chapter 6:

> *For we wrestle not against flesh and blood, but against principalities,* ***against powers, against the rulers of the darkness of this world, against spiritual wickedness in high places***.

The Law of the Land

I am no attorney or lawyer, so let's just see some facts and ask questions.

In the United States of America, defamation is not prosecutable at a federal level, because the First Amendment guarantees freedom of speech. However, most States have laws against defamation.

What is defamation? The Merriam-Webster online dictionary
states[154]:

> *the act of communicating false statements about a person that
> injure the reputation of that person: the act of defaming another:
> CALUMNY*

The Cornell Law School also offers a definition of defamation. It
states here[155]:

> *Defamation is a statement that injures a third party's reputation.
> The tort of defamation includes both libel (written statements)
> and slander (spoken statements).*

It also provides elements to prove the *prima facie* defamation. A
plaintiff would have to prove these following elements:

> 1) a false statement purporting to be fact.
> 2) publication or communication of that statement to a third
> person.
> 3) fault amounting to at least negligence; and
> 4) damages, or some harm caused to the person or entity who is
> the subject of the statement.

In the case of the authors of the ADL's report, can we already rule
out "truth" as a defense, and can negligence be thrown out the
window here, although not a defense?

Was the ADL's report published or communicated to a third
person[156]?

Do I really need to ask if the Honorable Minister Farrakhan has
suffered damages, or his family for that matter, by the ADL's report?

---

[154] From the Merriam-Webster online dictionary: https://www.merriam-
webster.com/dictionary/defamation.

[155] *Defamation*, Cornell Law School, Legal Information Institute:
https://www.law.cornell.edu/wex/defamation.

[156] *Farrakhan: In His Own Words*, ADL:
https://www.adl.org/education/resources/reports/nation-of-islam-farrakhan-in-his-own-words.

I believe it is now plain enough that a fool could understand why no one put his or her name on the ADL's report.

Some might wonder if suing the ADL would be appropriate. At the Hour the world of Satan is at, and considering the control he has over the judicial system, can justice be expected from it? It would be optimistic to believe so, and unnecessary because Allah states in the Holy Qur'an, chapter 3, verse 55:

> *When Allah said: **O Jesus, I will cause thee to die and exalt thee in My presence and clear thee of those who disbelieve** and make those who follow thee above those who disbelieve to the day of Resurrection. Then to Me is your return, so I shall decide between you concerning that wherein you differ.*

Who can be a better attorney and judge than Allah Himself?

The Scriptures

Jesus had a controversy with the (so-called) Jews. The book of John, chapter 8, relates the moment Jesus exposed the fake Jews, their plot, and its motive:

> *40 **But now ye seek to kill me, a man that hath told you the truth, which I have heard of God**: this did not Abraham.*

> *42 Jesus said unto them, **If God were your Father, ye would love me: for I proceeded forth and came from God**; neither came I of myself, but he sent me.*

> *43 Why do ye not understand my speech? even because ye cannot hear my word.*

> *44 **Ye are of your father the devil**, and the lusts of your father ye will do. **He was a murderer from the beginning, and abode not in the truth, because there is no truth in him**. When he speaketh a lie, he speaketh of his own: for he is a liar, and the father of it.*

*47 He that is of God heareth God's words: ye therefore hear them not, **because ye are not of God**.*

As the so-called Jews plan the death of a man, the Honorable Minister Farrakhan, who has sublime morals (Holy Qur'an chapter 68, verse 4), by attacking unjustly and wickedly his character, his integrity, his intentions, and the message of truth he delivers, the One God also plans. Holy Qur'an, chapter 3, verse 54:

And (the Jews) planned and Allah (also) planned. And Allah is the best of planners.

As written in the book of Matthew, chapter 27, verse 20, after the chief priests and the elders bring Jesus to Pontius Pilate to be judged, they and the people are offered a choice on who to release: Barabbas or Jesus. The verse states:

But the chief priests and elders persuaded the multitude that they should ask Barabbas, and destroy Jesus.

What was told to the people, whom earlier were crying "Hosanna to the Son of David" (Matthew 21: 9), that they would answer to Pilate in the book of Matthew chapter 27, verse 25?
... His blood be on us, and on our children.

Could it be that the chief priests and elders slandered Jesus, who committed no crime, to a point it would be justifiable for the people to see him die a horrible death, rather than to condemn Barabbas, a known murderer?

Now, the ADL's report, once properly analyzed and researched, is an evident slander towards the Honorable Minister Farrakhan.

Well, the Holy Qur'an has a chapter warning the slanderers in chapter 104:

In the name of Allah, the Beneficent, the Merciful.
*1 **Woe to every slanderer, defamer!***
2 Who amasses wealth and counts it—

3 He thinks that his wealth will make him abide.
*4 **Nay, he will certainly be hurled into the crushing disaster;***
5 And what will make thee realize what the crushing disaster is?
6 It is the Fire kindled by Allah,
7 Which rises over the hearts.
*8 **Surely it is closed in on them,***
9 In extended columns.

And we, who recognize the ADL for who they truly represent, can charge them of being slanderers of the Honorable Minister Farrakhan through their actions and words. They are hiding behind the good name of Judaism and claiming to be the Chosen ones. Well, if that is so, the Holy Qur'an has a challenge in chapter 2 verse 94:

Say: If the abode of the Hereafter with Allah is specially for you to the exclusion of the people, then invoke death if you are truthful.

We know they will not take that challenge, because the Holy Qur'an informs us in the following verse (95):

And they will never invoke it on account of what their hands have sent on before, and Allah knows the wrongdoers.

The Holy Qur'an, chapter 11, verse 18 states:

***And who is more <u>unjust</u> than he who forges a lie against Allah?** These will be brought before their Lord, **and the witnesses will say: These are they who lied against their Lord.** Now surely the curse of Allah is on the wrongdoers,*

I, and many others inside or outside the Nation of Islam, am a witness against the ADL of forging a lie against Allah. Indeed, by slandering the Honorable Minister Farrakhan, who is the mouthpiece of God. The book of John, chapter 1, verse 1:

*In the beginning was the **Word**, and the **Word** was with God, **and the Word was God.***

Further evidence in chapter 8, verses 26, 28, 29, 38 and 58:

*26 I have many things to say and to judge of you: but he that sent me is true; **and I speak to the world those things which I have heard of him**.*

*28 Then said Jesus unto them, When ye have lifted up the Son of man, then shall ye know that I am he, and that I do nothing of myself; **but as my Father hath taught me, I speak these things**.*

*29 **And he that sent me is with me**: the Father hath not left me alone; for I do always those things that please him.*

*38 **I speak that which I have seen with my Father**: and ye do that which ye have seen with your father.*
*58 Jesus said unto them, Verily, verily, I say unto you, **Before Abraham was, I am.***

So, for your slander of the Word of God, ADL, but especially on how you and your brethren do it, Allah sends down from Heaven a pestilence. This was explained by the Honorable Minister Farrakhan on July 4th, 2020. He mentioned two verses in the Holy Qur'an. Chapter 2, verse 59 and chapter 7, verse 162:

*2:59 **But those who were <u>unjust</u> changed the word which had been spoken to them, for another saying**, so We sent upon the wrongdoers a pestilence from heaven, because they transgressed.*

*7:162 **But those who were <u>unjust</u> among them changed it for a word other than that which they were told**, so We sent upon them a pestilence from heaven for their wrongdoing.*

The pestilence mentioned is the coronavirus. The wisdom of this unraveling world will not prevail against the wisdom of Allah (God).

The time of respite given to Iblis (Satan) as mentioned in the Holy Qur'an, chapter 7, verses 14 and 15, has come to an end.

Either ADL you clean up your act very soon, or you can expect from the Lord of hosts what is written in the book of Malachi, chapter 4, verse 1:

For, behold, the day cometh, that shall burn as an oven; and all the proud, yea, and all that do wickedly, shall be stubble: and the day that cometh shall burn them up, saith the Lord of hosts, that it shall leave them neither root nor branch.

The Door to Repentance

This last section of the book is a call to repentance for those who participated and participate in the slander of the Honorable Minister Farrakhan. As long as the doom has not come, the door to repentance is still opened, but closing very soon.

The Supreme Being has the best attributes. One of which being the Most Merciful. Indeed, were it not for His Mercy, the Holy Qur'an states in chapter 16, verse 61:

And if Allah were to destroy men for their iniquity, He would not leave therein a single creature, *but He respites them till an appointed time. So when their doom comes, they are not able to delay (it) an hour, nor can they advance (it).*

While there is still time, we must turn back to the Most High. I write "we" because the previous verse informs us that we are all guilty of iniquity and the only reason we are still breathing is from His Mercy. But how?

The Holy Qur'an, chapter 4, verses 17 and 18:

*17 **Repentance with Allah is only for those who do evil in ignorance, then turn (to Allah) soon**, so these it is to whom Allah turns (mercifully). And Allah is ever Knowing, Wise.*

*18 **And repentance is not for those who go on doing evil deeds, until when death comes to one of them, he says: Now I repent;***

nor (for) those who die while they are disbelievers. *For such We have prepared a painful chastisement.*

During the historic message by the Honorable Minister Farrakhan, on July 4th, 2020, The Criterion, he made a call for repentance. He said[157]:

> ***So, if you really want to end the virus***, *Mr. Xi, recall your sins. Don't tell me presidents don't have sin. Go and lis…* ***go in your chamber and look at your record***. *Have you sinned? Is there anyone in here that has not sinned? Raise your hand. Oh! I didn't see nobody. I can't say that I have not sinned. But I can say with truth that God has taken care of my sins.* ***So, the Scripture says: "Pray to me and I will forgive you." The God will forgive you.*** *When I leave, he said he will not punish you while I'm among you.* ***But he won't punish you if you're in the middle of repentance!*** *So now that you know your sins, and COVID is spiking… I don't know how many States are seeing the spike. How many? 36? No, you're not keeping up with the news. It's more like 40, going toward 50. Nobody is going to escape. You haven't seen the worse of this yet. When I close down in the garden, the God will do some work.*
>
> *(…)*
>
> ***So, this pestilence is gonna get worse.*** *But you! But America! But China! If you don't want to get caught up in the next phase of the blowing of the Trumpet, then* ***what you should do is call you people together and come out to them and ask them to go in their chambers of quiet and ask forgiveness for your sins. For your sins have reached unto Heaven.***

So, to whoever participated in the writing of the ADL's defamatory report, know that you have sinned a great sin. Repentance is prescribed.

---

[157] The Criterion, starting at 1 hour 59 minutes 31 seconds, then jump to the mark of 2 hour 25 minutes and 46 seconds: https://media.noi.org/watch/the-criterion-rebroadcast.

To end this volume, since you claim to be Jews, let us read from the book of Daniel, the prayer for the Jews, chapter 9, verses 3-19:

3 And I set my face unto the Lord God, to seek by prayer and supplications, with fasting, and sackcloth, and ashes:

4 And I prayed unto the Lord my God, and made my confession, and said, O Lord, the great and dreadful God, keeping the covenant and mercy to them that love him, and to them that keep his commandments;

5 We have sinned, and have committed iniquity, and have done wickedly, and have rebelled, even by departing from thy precepts and from thy judgments:

6 Neither have we hearkened unto thy servants the prophets, which spake in thy name to our kings, our princes, and our fathers, and to all the people of the land.

7 O Lord, righteousness belongeth unto thee, but unto us confusion of faces, as at this day; to the men of Judah, and to the inhabitants of Jerusalem, and unto all Israel, that are near, and that are far off, through all the countries whither thou hast driven them, because of their trespass that they have trespassed against thee.

8 O Lord, to us belongeth confusion of face, to our kings, to our princes, and to our fathers, because we have sinned against thee.

9 To the Lord our God belong mercies and forgivenesses, though we have rebelled against him;

10 Neither have we obeyed the voice of the Lord our God, to walk in his laws, which he set before us by his servants the prophets.

11 Yea, all Israel have transgressed thy law, even by departing, that they might not obey thy voice; therefore the curse is poured upon us, and the oath that is written in the law of Moses the servant of God, because we have sinned against him.

12 And he hath confirmed his words, which he spake against us, and against our judges that judged us, by bringing upon us a great evil: for under the whole heaven hath not been done as hath been done upon Jerusalem.

13 As it is written in the law of Moses, all this evil is come upon us: yet made we not our prayer before the Lord our God, that we might turn from our iniquities, and understand thy truth.

14 Therefore hath the Lord watched upon the evil, and brought it upon us: for the Lord our God is righteous in all his works which he doeth: for we obeyed not his voice.

15 And now, O Lord our God, that hast brought thy people forth out of the land of Egypt with a mighty hand, and hast gotten thee renown, as at this day; we have sinned, we have done wickedly.

16 O Lord, according to all thy righteousness, I beseech thee, let thine anger and thy fury be turned away from thy city Jerusalem, thy holy mountain: because for our sins, and for the iniquities of our fathers, Jerusalem and thy people are become a reproach to all that are about us.

17 Now therefore, O our God, hear the prayer of thy servant, and his supplications, and cause thy face to shine upon thy sanctuary that is desolate, for the Lord's sake.

18 O my God, incline thine ear, and hear; open thine eyes, and behold our desolations, and the city which is called by thy name: for we do not present our supplications before thee for our righteousnesses, but for thy great mercies.

19 O Lord, hear; O Lord, forgive; O Lord, hearken and do; defer not, for thine own sake, O my God: for thy city and thy people are called by thy name.

End of volume 1

Bibliography

Books, lectures, online articles, online sources

1946 King David Hotel Bombing. (2018, August 14). YouTube. https://www.youtube.com/watch?v=7lFayd9TWa0. Last accessed August 21, 2021.

5 Dancing Israelis. (2019, October 6). YouTube. https://www.youtube.com/watch?v=yLnKiTmO64c. Last accessed August 21, 2021.

Abrams, Nathan. *Nathan Abrams on Jews in the American Porn Industry.* Scribd. https://www.scribd.com/document/135073670/Nathan-Abrams-on-Jews-in-the-American-Porn-Industry. Last accessed August 24, 2021.

Adams, Thelma. *Casting-Couch Tactics Plagued Hollywood Long Before Harvey Weinstein.* (2017, October 17). Variety. https://variety.com/2017/film/features/casting-couch-hollywood-sexual-harassment-harvey-weinstein-1202589895/. Last accessed August 25, 2021.

ADL: Anti-Semitism Around Leo Frank Case Flourishes on 100th Anniversary. Anti-Defamation League. https://www.adl.org/news/press-releases/adl-anti-semitism-around-leo-frank-case-flourishes-on-100th-anniversary. Last accessed August 21, 2021.

ADL head calls on Barack Obama to again denounce Louis Farrakhan. (2018, January 31). Jewish Telegraphic Agency. https://www.jta.org/2018/01/31/united-states/adl-head-calls-on-barack-obama-to-again-denounce-louis-farrakhan. Last accessed August 21, 2021.

ADL Urges Tuskegee University President: Repudiate Hate Speech of Louis Farrakhan Before Campus Visit. (2013. March 14). ADL. https://atlanta.adl.org/adl-urges-tuskegee-university-president-repudiate-hate-speech-of-louis-farrakhan-before-campus-visit/. Last accessed August 21, 2021.

Arnold, Paul. *Too Short Says There Was An Industry-Wide Plot To Shut Down Conscious Hip Hop.* (2012, February 29). HipHopDX. https://hiphopdx.com/news/id.18861/title.too-short-says-there-was-an-industry-wide-plot-to-shut-down-conscious-hip-hop#. Last accessed August 25, 2021.

Associated Press. *Who are top 5 donors to Obama, Romney campaigns?.* (2012, October 19). POLITICO. https://www.politico.com/story/2012/10/who-are-top-5-donors-to-obama-romney-campaigns-082637. Last accessed August 21, 2021.

AUDIO INTERVIEW: 9–11 Cop Who Arrested Dancing Israelis Speaks. (2011, October 14). American Free Press. https://americanfreepress.net/9-11-cop-who-arrested-dancing-israelis-speaks/. Last accessed August 22, 2021.

Bailey, Ian. *Bronfman heiresses accused of crucial financing of sex cult NXIVM in lawsuit.* (2020, February 12). The Globe and Mail. https://www.theglobeandmail.com/canada/british-columbia/article-sara-clare-bronfman-named-in-us-lawsuit-against-sex-cult-nxivm/. Last accessed August 22, 2021.

Barack Obama Top Contributors, 2008 Cycle. Opensecrets.org. https://www.opensecrets.org/pres08/contrib.php?cid=n00009638. Last accessed August 25, 2021.

Bernstein, Jay. *Morgan leadership must denounce Farrakhan's appearance.* (2014, November 19). The Baltimore Sun. https://www.baltimoresun.com/opinion/op-ed/bs-ed-farrakhan-morgan-20141119-story.html. Last accessed August 22, 2021.

Boyarsky, Bill & Clayton, *Janet. Bradley Promised Silence on Farrakhan to Black Leaders.* (1985, September 13). Los Angeles Times. https://www.latimes.com/archives/la-xpm-1985-09-13-me-22471-story.html. Last accessed August 22, 2021.

Brackman, Dr. Harold. *Louis Farrakhan – Four Decades of Bigotry In His Own Words.* (2020, June). Simon Wiesenthal Center. https://www.wiesenthal.com/assets/pdf/new-swc-report-farrakhan.pdf?fbclid=IwAR0w4bmYjBkpMV_pApvouEqqGmqzfd2LQYNOm6Eq2d8H-Br_MHiRX5Cp-74. Last accessed August 21, 2021.
________ *Ministry of Lies: The Truth Behind The Secret Relationship Between Blacks and Jews.* (1994, September 14). Goodreads. https://www.goodreads.com/book/show/438697.Ministry_of_Lies. Last accessed August 21, 2021.

Clark, A. *Bankers and academics at top of donor list.* (2008, November 8). The Guardian. https://www.theguardian.com/world/2008/nov/08/barackobama-wallstreet-bankers-campaign-donations-goldmansachs. Last accessed August 21, 2021.

Congressional Record—House. (1877, March 1). Govinfo. https://www.govinfo.gov/content/pkg/GPO-CRECB-1877-pt3-v5/pdf/GPO-CRECB-1877-pt3-v5-9-2.pdf. Last accessed August 21, 2021.

Constitution of the state of Louisiana, adopted in convention at . . . New Orleans, the twenty-third day of July, A.D. 1879. (1879). Internet Archive. https://archive.org/details/constitutionsta00louigoog/page/n51/mode/2up?q=american. Last accessed August 21, 2021.

Defamation. LII / Legal Information Institute. Cornell Law School. https://www.law.cornell.edu/wex/defamation. Last accessed August 21, 2021.

Dror, Yuval. *Odigo Says Workers Were Warned of Attack.* (2001, September 26). Haaretz. https://www.haaretz.com/1.5410231. Last accessed August 21, 2021.

Ehud Barak Is Real Terrorist - BBC Interview - Date 9/11/2001. (2012, April 4). YouTube. https://www.youtube.com/watch?app=desktop&v=TFEgBCrBb1Y. Last accessed August 21, 2021.

Ezekiel, Herbert T. *19 May 1899, Page 8*. (1899, May 9). The Jewish South. The Jewish South. Volume 11, Number 19. https://www.newspapers.com/image/89033324/. Last accessed August 21, 2021.
______. *24 June 1898, Page 6*. (1898, June 24). The Jewish South. Volume 9, Number 24. https://www.newspapers.com/image/89032900/?terms=negroes. Last accessed August 21, 2021.

Farrakhan @ Tuskegee University, Exposing The U.S. Government on Campus. (2013, March 26). YouTube. https://www.youtube.com/watch?app=desktop&v=SM63OMZQDmI. Last accessed August 21, 2021.

Farrakhan: In His Own Words. (2015, March 20). Anti-Defamation League. https://www.adl.org/sites/default/files/documents/assets/pdf/anti-semitism/united-states/farrakhan-in-his-own-words-2015-03-20.pdf. Last accessed August 21, 2021.

Farrakhan: In His Own Words. Anti-Defamation League. https://www.adl.org/education/resources/reports/nation-of-islam-farrakhan-in-his-own-words. Last accessed August 21, 2021.

Farrakhan, Minister Louis. *7 Speeches*. (1992). WKU and The Final Call Inc.
______. *How Strong Is Our Foundation; Can We Survive?-Saviours' Day 2014*. (2014, February 23). The Final Call Online Store. https://finalcallstore.noi.org/product/how-strong-is-our-foundation-can-we-survive-saviours-day-2014-dvd/. Last accessed August 21, 2021.
______. *How Strong Is Our Foundation: Can We Survive? Part 2*. (2014, March 2). The Final Call Online Store. https://finalcallstore.noi.org/product/how-strong-is-our-foundation-can-we-survive-part-2-dvd/. Last accessed August 21, 2021.
______. *Saviours' Day 2015 Pt. 2: The Intensifying Universal Cry for Justice*. (2015, March 1). The Final Call Online Store. https://finalcallstore.noi.org/product/saviours-day-2015-pt-2-the-intensifying-universal-cry-for-justice-dvd/. Last accessed August 25, 2021.
______. *Saviours' Day 2018 Keynote Address*. (2018, February 25). The Final Call Online Store. https://finalcallstore.noi.org/product/saviours-day-2018-keynote-address/. Last accessed August 24, 2021.
______. *The Criterion*. (2020, July 4th). Nation of Islam. https://media.noi.org/watch/the-criterion-rebroadcast. Last accessed August 24, 2021.
______. *The Time And What Must Be Done, Detroit*. (2013, May 17). The Final Call Online Store. https://finalcallstore.noi.org/product/the-time-and-what-must-be-done-detroit-dvd/. Last accessed August 25, 2021.
______. *The Time And What Must Be Done Pt 20*. The Final Call Online Store. https://finalcallstore.noi.org/product/the-time-and-what-must-be-done-pt-20-dvd/. Last accessed August 25, 2021.

________. *Tuskegee University: The Seminal Fluid Of The Kingdom Of God.* (2013, March 22). The Final Call Online Store. https://finalcallstore.noi.org/product/tuskegee-university-the-seminal-fluid-of-the-kingdom-of-god-dvd/. Last accessed August 25, 2021.

Federal Reserve Board - Federal Reserve Act. Board of Governors of the Federal Reserve System. https://www.federalreserve.gov/aboutthefed/fract.htm. Last accessed August 21, 2021.

Fox News: Israeli Spy Ring Operating In America. (2014, September 11). YouTube. https://www.youtube.com/watch?app=desktop&v=9J-eAtxX7l0. Last accessed August 21, 2021.

Frank, Dr. Herman. *Judah P. Benjamin and the Ku Klux Klan.* (1925, October 9). The Detroit Jewish Chronicle News Digital Archives. https://digital.bentley.umich.edu/djnews/djc.1925.10.09.001/6?fbclid=IwAR0Xxk9eIlWHaV01roH1i1j8xD2aKlp9O9H3QCw54yGp9dBP_RG9Ttejst4. Last accessed August 21, 2021.

Freedman, Harry. *Babylonian Talmud: Tractate Sanhedrin.* Halakah. http://halakhah.com/sanhedrin/sanhedrin_106.html. Last accessed August 25, 2021.

Freidman, Manny. *Jews Do Control the Media.* (2012, July 3). Algemeiner.Com. https://www.algemeiner.com/2012/07/03/jews-do-control-the-media/?fbclid=IwAR1ae7vYNnRXty-JzFdIWNnsvv4qDu3fBHfCCWja18gPUL0hNIaJtz81lZs. Last accessed August 24, 2021.

Ghose, Tia. *Surprise: Ashkenazi Jews Are Genetically European.* (2013, October 8). Live Science. https://www.livescience.com/40247-ashkenazi-jews-have-european-genes.html. Last accessed August 25, 2021.

Government - Historical Debt Outstanding - Annual 1900 - 1949. TreasuryDirect. https://www.treasurydirect.gov/govt/reports/pd/histdebt/histdebt_histo3.htm. Last accessed August 21, 2021.

Haaretz Service & Reuters. *Report: Netanyahu says 9/11 terror attacks good for Israel.* (2008, April 15). Haaretz. https://www.haaretz.com/1.4970678. Last accessed August 25, 2021.

Henry Ford Invents a Jewish Conspiracy. Jewish Virtual Library. https://www.jewishvirtuallibrary.org/henry-ford-invents-a-jewish-conspiracy. Last accessed August 21, 2021.

Holy Bible, King James Version. Thomas Nelson.

Hurtado, Patricia. *Weinstein Prosecutors Build Case That Casting Couch Was Trap.* (2020, January 29). Bloomberg. https://www.bloomberg.com/news/articles/2020-01-29/weinstein-casting-couch-could-save-him-or-send-him-to-prison. Last accessed August 25, 2021.

Jarvis, Rebecca & al. *"Hot Girls Wanted": How Teen Girls Seeking Fame Can Be Lured into Amateur Porn*. (2015, June 4). ABC News. https://abcnews.go.com/US/hot-girls-wanted-teen-girls-seeking-fame-lured/story?id=31290984. Last accessed August 25, 2021.

Jerusalem Post Staff. *Simon Wiesenthal Center condemns Farrakhan's July 4th speech on Revolt TV*. (2020, July 6). The Jerusalem Post. https://www.jpost.com/diaspora/antisemitism/simon-wiesenthal-center-condemns-farrakhans-july-4th-speech-on-revolt-tv-634010?fbclid=IwAR1MAkpHR6aqlTVtSWBiQHkTE1ZQMCsAWFR0OqztUqc5hU3VJsxiGrmx7i0. Last accessed August 21, 2021.

Joel Spingarn Attacks Dr. Washington. (1914, February 26). The New York Age. Newspapers.com. https://www.newspapers.com/image/?clipping_id=25865880&fcfToken=eyJhbGciOiJIUzI1NiIsInR5cCI6IkpXVCJ9.eyJmcmVlLXZpZXctaWQiOjMzNDYyNjM0LCJpYXQiOjE2Mjk2ODg0MTUsImV4cCI6MTYyOTc3NDgxNX0.gge0_grlZwIru6C8Y0kz9wp2ebh7w6X3uHr6-zSLr8Q. Last accessed August 22, 2021.

Joel Spingarn. Jewish Virtual Library. https://www.jewishvirtuallibrary.org/joel-spingarn. Last accessed August 22, 2021.

Joyce, Fay S. *JACKSON CRITICIZES REMARKS MADE BY FARRAKHAN AS "REPREHENSIBLE."*. (1984, June 29). The New York Times. https://www.nytimes.com/1984/06/29/world/jackson-criticizes-remarks-made-by-farrakhan-as-reprehensible.html. Last accessed August 21, 2021.

Joyce, Kathleen. *Porn star sues company, director and performer for alleged sexual battery*. (2018, April 10). New York Post. https://nypost.com/2018/04/10/porn-star-sues-company-director-and-performer-for-alleged-sexual-battery/. Last accessed August 24, 2021.

Judah Benjamin. Jewish Virtual Library. https://www.jewishvirtuallibrary.org/judah-benjamin. Last accessed August 25, 2021.

Kampeas, Ron. *What was Louis Farrakhan doing at that Congressional Black Caucus meeting with Obama? Here's what we found out*. (2018, February 1). Jewish Telegraphic Agency. https://www.jta.org/2018/02/01/politics/what-was-louis-farrakhan-doing-at-a-congressional-black-caucus-meeting. Last accessed August 25, 2021.

Ketcham, Christopher. *The Israeli "art student" mystery*. (2002, May 7). Salon. https://www.salon.com/2002/05/07/students/. Last accessed August 21, 2021.

Kissinger, Heinz (Henry). *National Security Study Memorandum 200: Implications of Worldwide Population Growth for U.S. Security and Overseas Interests*. (1974, April 24). https://pdf.usaid.gov/pdf_docs/PCAAB500.pdf. Last accessed June 2021.

Klansmen present wreath to Jew. (1924, September 2). The Evening Republican.
    Newspapers.com.
    https://www.newspapers.com/image/?clipping_id=24913758&fcfToken=eyJhb
    GciOiJIUzI1NiIsInR5cCI6IkpXVCJ9.eyJmcmVlLXZpZXctaWQiOjEzMDk3M
    zYyOCwiaWF0IjoxNjI5ODQyODcxLCJleHAiOjE2Mjk5MjkyNzF9.ZsrdbSPu
    q3tV4lK4JTLIk6EsLkQVsQs5-FhdXGetyrA. Last accessed August 24, 2021.

Knutsen, E. *Israel Forcibly Injected African Immigrants with Birth Control,
    Report Claims*. (2013, January 28). Forbes.
    https://www.forbes.com/sites/eliseknutsen/2013/01/28/israel-foribly-injected-
    african-immigrant-women-with-birth-control/#26709a2767b8. Last accessed
    August 21, 2021.

Koestler, Arthur. *The Thirteenth Tribe*. (1976).
    http://www.fantompowa.info/13th%20Tribe.pdf. Last accessed August 21, 2021.

*Louisiana State Museum Online Exhibits The Cabildo: Two Centuries of
    Louisiana History – Reconstruction I: A State Divided*. Louisiana.
    https://www.crt.state.la.us/louisiana-state-museum/online-exhibits/the-
    cabildo/reconstruction-a-state-divided/index. Last accessed August 24, 2021.

Leibovich-Dar, Sara. *Up in smoke*. (2001, November 20). Haaretz.
    https://www.haaretz.com/1.5462012. Last accessed August 25, 2021.

Lindemann, Albert S. *The Jew Accused: three anti-Semitic affaires (Dreyfus,
    Beilis, Frank, 1894-1915*. (1991). Cambridge University Press. Google Books:
    https://books.google.ca/books?id=YCugGyqkYBQC&printsec=frontcover&dq=t
    he+jew+accused+books&hl=en&sa=X&ved=2ahUKEwidnqHYmb3sAhVDgnI
    EHQZsDwwQ6AEwAHoECAIQAg#v=onepage&q=the%20jew%20accused%2
    0books&f=false. Last accessed August 21, 2021.

Leo. *Emasculating The Black Male: 15 Actors Who Wore a Dress For Success*.
    (2013, November 6). Atlanta Black Star.
    https://atlantablackstar.com/2013/11/05/emasculating-the-black-male-15-actors-
    who-wore-a-dress-for-success/. Last accessed August 24, 2021.

MacKinnon, Catharine A., *Pornography as Trafficking*. (2005). Michigan Journal
    of International Law. Volume 26, Issue 4.
    https://repository.law.umich.edu/cgi/viewcontent.cgi?article=1241&context=mji
    l. Last accessed August 21, 2021.

Maddaus, Gene. *Harvey Weinstein Loses Bid to Toss Sex Trafficking Claim*.
    (2019, December 19). Variety. https://variety.com/2019/biz/news/harvey-
    weinstein-sex-trafficking-count-1203449388/. Last accessed August 21, 2021.

Manchester, Julian. *Jewish GOP group calls on Dem lawmakers to resign over
    Farrakhan remarks*. (2018, March 6). The Hill. https://thehill.com/blogs/blog-
    briefing-room/news/377053-jewish-gop-group-calls-on-lawmakers-tied-to-
    farrakhan-to-resign. Last accessed August 24, 2021.

Merida, Kevin. *BLACK LEADERS CALL ON FARRAKHAN TO REPUDIATE CONTROVERSIAL REMARKS BY AIDE*. (1994, January 26). Washington Post. https://www.washingtonpost.com/archive/politics/1994/01/26/black-leaders-call-on-farrakhan-to-repudiate-controversial-remarks-by-aide/6c057641-c259-4803-92b2-d7fd06d27d9d/. Last accessed August 24, 2021.

Merriam-Webster. The Merriam-Webster.Com Dictionary. https://www.merriam-webster.com/.

Minister Farrakhan "Sets The Record Straight." (2016, April 10). YouTube. https://www.youtube.com/watch?app=desktop&v=kJOPkx9eozY. Last accessed August 24, 2021.

Minister Farrakhan - Response to Facebook. (2019, May 10). YouTube. https://www.youtube.com/watch?v=3nvaUB1qIfE. Last accessed August 25, 2021.

Monthly Statement of the Public Debt of the United States. (2013, December 31). TreasuryDirect. https://www.treasurydirect.gov/govt/reports/pd/mspd/2013/opds122013.pdf. Last accessed August 24, 2021.

"Mothers of all Palestinians should also be killed," says Israeli politician. (2014, July 14). Daily Sabah. https://www.dailysabah.com/mideast/2014/07/14/mothers-of-all-palestinians-should-also-be-killed-says-israeli-politician. Last accessed August 21, 2021.

Muhammad, Abdul Arif, *A Response to Alan Dershowitz, Esq. 'YOU ARE OF YOUR FATHER THE DEVIL (SATAN).'* (2020, July 9). The Final Call. https://www.mydigitalpublication.com/publication/?i=667008&article_id=3718791&view=articleBrowser. Last accessed August 21, 2021.

Muhammad, Askia. *MUHAMMAD: The Censorship of Louis Farrakhan*. (2020, July 15). The Washington Informer. https://www.washingtoninformer.com/muhammad-the-censorship-of-louis-farrakhan/. Last accessed August 21, 2021.

Muhammad, Ebony Safiyyah. *LGBTQ opposition to Dr. Wesley Muhammad rises*. (2017, December 6). The Final Call. https://www.finalcall.com/artman/publish/National_News_2/article_103909.shtml. Last accessed August 21, 2021.

Muhammad, Jabril. *Closing the Gap*, Chicago, Il: FNC Publishing Co., 2006, p. 365.

Muhammad Ali, Maulana. English Translation of *The Holy Qur'an*. (2008, November) Second Printing. Ahmadiyya Anjuman Isha'at Islam Lahore Inc.

Nation of Islam. *Confessions of a Jewish Racist: Dr. Harold Brackman*. (2016, August 11). Nation of Islam Research Group. https://noirg.org/articles/confessions-of-a-jewish-racist-dr-harold-brackman/. Last accessed August 24, 2021.
_______. *The Controversy with the Jews: What is the Truth?*. (2020, July 21). The

Final Call. https://new.finalcall.com/2020/07/21/the-controversy-with-the-jews-what-is-the-truth/. Last accessed August 24, 2021.

________. *The Secret Relationship Between Blacks and Jews*. Vol. 1. Chicago: Nation of Islam. 1991.

________. *The Secret Relationship Between Blacks and Jews*. Vol. 2. *How Jews Gained Control of the Black American Economy*. 2nd ed. Chicago: Nation of Islam. 2010.

________. *The Secret Relationship Between Blacks and Jews*. Vol. 3. *The Leo Frank Case – The Lynching of a Guilty Man*. Chicago: Nation of Islam. 2016.

Our Values. ADL. https://www.adl.org/who-we-are/our-values. Last accessed August 25, 2021.

Palestine 1946: King David Hotel Bomb Warning Controversy. (2008, April 12). YouTube. https://www.youtube.com/watch?app=desktop&v=4ZHHTjuv5jc. Last accessed August 25, 2021.

Rabbis Thank Neturei Karta for "Unmistakable Proof" of Anti-Semitism in Congress. (2021, March 19). Coalition for. Coalition for Jewish Values. https://coalitionforjewishvalues.org/2019/03/rabbis-thank-neturei-karta-for-unmistakable-proof-of-anti-semitism-in-congress/. Last accessed August 21, 2021.

Remembering Leo Frank. ADL. https://www.adl.org/resources/backgrounders/remembering-leo-frank. Last accessed August 25, 2021.

Remnick, David. *The Lobby*. (2007, August 27). The New Yorker. https://www.newyorker.com/magazine/2007/09/03/the-lobby. Last accessed August 21, 2021.

Rodkinson, Michael L. *The Babylonian Talmud*. (1918). https://www.jewishvirtuallibrary.org/jsource/Judaism/FullTalmud.pdf. Last accessed August 24, 2021.

Rothstein, Arnold. Jewish Virtual Library. https://www.jewishvirtuallibrary.org/arnold-rothstein. Last accessed August 21, 2021.

Ruiz, Karen, & Wright, Matthew. *At least 100 more women come forward with claims against GirlsDoPorn scheme*. (2020, January 7) Daily Mail Online. https://www.dailymail.co.uk/news/article-7858901/At-100-women-come-forward-claims-against-GirlsDoPorn-scheme.html. Last accessed August 24, 2021.

Sachar, Howard. *Jews in the Civil Rights Movement*. (2004, August 31). My Jewish Learning. https://www.myjewishlearning.com/article/jews-in-the-civil-rights-movement/. https://www.myjewishlearning.com/article/jews-in-the-civil-rights-movement/. Last accessed August 21, 2021.

Saengian, Kathy. *Researcher cites negative influences of hip-hop*. (2008, June 13). Pittsburgh Post-Gazette. https://www.post-gazette.com/life/lifestyle/2008/06/13/Researcher-cites-negative-influences-of-hip-hop/stories/200806130124. Last accessed August 24, 2021.

Saker Woeste, Victoria. *Why Ford needs to grapple with its founder's anti-Semitism*. (2019, February 9). The Washington Post. https://www.washingtonpost.com/outlook/2019/02/08/why-ford-needs-grapple-with-its-founders-anti-semitism/. Last accessed August 25, 2021.

Salisbury, Stephan. *Jewish groups call for ouster of local NAACP head over anti-Semitic Facebook post*. (2020, July 25). The Philadelphia Inquirer. https://www.inquirer.com/news/rodney-muhammad-naacp-anti-semitic-jewish-federation-adl-20200725.html. Last accessed August 25, 2021.

Saphire, William. *Black Muslim Leader Extols Hitler*. (1984, April 13). Jewish Telegraphic Agency. http://pdfs.jta.org/1984/1984-04-13_072.pdf?_ga=2.22030331.1582539831.1598758837-1241064722.1595383865. Last accessed August 25, 2021.

Schmalz, Jeffrey. *INVITATION TO FARRAKHAN CAUSES RIFT AT WESLEYAN*. (1984, October 9). The New York Times. https://www.nytimes.com/1984/10/09/nyregion/invitation-to-farrakhan-causes-rift-at-wesleyan.html. Last accessed August 22, 2021.

Scott v. Federal Reserve Bank of Kansas City. (2005, April 28). FindLaw for legal professionals. https://caselaw.findlaw.com/us-8th-circuit/1208321.html. Last accessed August 25, 2021.

Silverman, Eric. *Sex Trafficking Is a Jewish Issue*. (2019, May 22). JewishBoston. https://www.jewishboston.com/read/sex-trafficking-is-a-jewish-issue/. Last accessed August 21, 2021.

Stein, Joel. *Who runs Hollywood? C'mon*. (2019, March 1). Los Angeles Times. https://www.latimes.com/archives/la-xpm-2008-dec-19-oe-stein19-story.html. Last accessed August 25, 2021.

Stevens, William K. *In Tense Times at Penn, Enter Farrakhan*. (1988, April 11). The New York Times. https://www.nytimes.com/1988/04/11/us/in-tense-times-at-penn-enter-farrakhan.html. Last accessed August 25, 2021.

Reich, Kenneth & Paddock, Richard C. Paddock. *Civil Rights Groups Sue ADL, Ask for Injunction Against Spying : Court: Plaintiffs say that law enforcement authorities allowed confidential files to be given to the Jewish anti-extremism organization*. (1993, October 22). Los Angeles Times. https://www.latimes.com/archives/la-xpm-1993-10-22-me-48538-story.html. Last accessed August 24, 2021.

Syracuse Group Refuses to Cut Off Funds for Farrakhan Talk. (November 8, 1987). The New York Times. https://www.nytimes.com/1987/11/08/nyregion/syracuse-group-refuses-to-cut-off-funds-for-farrakhan-talk.html. Last accessed August 21, 2021.

The 4,000 Jews Rumor. International Information Programs. Internet Archive Wayback Machine. https://web.archive.org/web/20050408072925/http:/usinfo.state.gov/media/Archive/2005/Jan/14-260933.html. Last accessed August 25, 2021.

The FBI and the Anti-Defamation League. The Israel Lobby Archive – The Institute for Research: Middle Eastern Policy. https://www.israellobby.org/ADL/. Last accessed August 25, 2021.

The Jerusalem Post Internet Staff. *Hundreds of Israelis missing in WTC attack*. (2001, September 12). The Internet Jerusalem Post. Internet Archive Wayback Machine. https://web.archive.org/web/20050412040213/http:/www.fpp.co.uk/online/02/10/JerusPost120901.html. Last accessed August 22, 2021.

The Nation of Islam. *FBI COINTELPRO: The U.S. Government's War Against Dissent*. (2020, January 3). NOI.Org Official Website. https://www.noi.org/cointelpro/. Last accessed August 21, 2021.
_______. *FBI COINTELPRO - Aug. 25, 1967*. (2019, April 24). NOI.Org Official Website. https://www.noi.org/fbi_08-25-1967/. Last accessed August 21, 2021.

The New Negro Movement - NAACP: A Century in the Fight for Freedom. Library of Congress. https://www.loc.gov/exhibits/naacp/the-new-negro-movement.html. Last accessed August 22, 2021.

Tobacco Trade and Industries. Encyclopedia. https://www.encyclopedia.com/religion/encyclopedias-almanacs-transcripts-and-maps/tobacco-trade-and-industries. Last accessed August 22, 2021.

Victims of Trafficking and Violence Protection Act of 2000. (2000, October 28). GovInfo. https://www.govinfo.gov/content/pkg/PLAW-106publ386/pdf/PLAW-106publ386.pdf. Last accessed August 25, 2021.

Welch, Will. *Pharrell on Evolving Masculinity, "Blurred Lines," and "Spiritual Warfare."* (2019, October 14). GQ. https://www.gq.com/story/pharrell-new-masculinity-cover-interview. Last accessed August 25, 2021.

Weiss, Rabbi Stewart M. `THE BLACKS MUST REPUDIATE FARRAKHAN`. (1985, December 28). Chicago Tribune. https://www.chicagotribune.com/news/ct-xpm-1985-12-28-8503300345-story.html. Last accessed August 25, 2021.

Were Israelis Detained on Sept. 11 Spies?. (2006, January 6). ABC News. https://abcnews.go.com/2020/story?id=123885&page=1. Last accessed August 25, 2021.

"When the sun rises in the west; Saviours' Day '90". (2014, September 13). YouTube. https://www.youtube.com/watch?app=desktop&v=KoNPoQmhNyQ. Last accessed August 25, 2021.

William Mallory Levy. Jewish Virtual Library. https://www.jewishvirtuallibrary.org/william-mallory-levy. Last accessed August 25, 2021.

Virtual Jewish World: Recife, Brazil. Jewish Virtual Library.
https://www.jewishvirtuallibrary.org/recife-brazil. Last accessed August 25, 2021.

Volume 6: Federal Bureau of Investigation. Assassination Archives and Research Center.
https://www.aarclibrary.org/publib/church/reports/vol6/html/ChurchV6_0200a.htm. Last accessed August 25, 2021.

Index

Buddhism, 49

C

D

E

Hayes, Rutherford B., 24, 25
Hebrew Globe Newspaper, The, 92
Hirsch, Steven, 72
Hitler, 37
Hot Girls Wanted, 73

I

Irgun, 57, 58
Islam, 45, 48, 59
Israel, 10, 13, 31, 32, 34, 36, 42, 43, 45, 46, 49, 50, 51, 52, 53, 54, 55, 56, 58, 106
    5 dancing Israelis, 54, 55
    Army, 9
    Government, 13, 53, 54, 56
    MOSSAD, 53, 56
    Nation, 31
    Police, 9
    Spy ring, 52

J

Jackson, Brandon T., 84
Jackson, Reverend Jesse, 17, 18, 19, 20, 37
Jeremy, Ron, 72
Jerusalem Post, The, 40, 56
Jew, 4, 5, 6, 7, 8, 9, 10, 11, 12, 13, 15, 16, 17, 22, 23, 27, 28, 29, 30, 33, 34, 35, 38, 39, 45, 46, 47, 48, 49, 50, 51, 56, 57, 58, 59, 60, 61, 62, 63, 64, 66, 67, 68, 70, 72, 73, 74, 75, 78, 79, 80, 82, 83, 84, 85, 89, 90, 91, 92, 93, 94, 95, 96, 98, 100, 101, 106
    Ashkenazi, 9, 13, 46, 47
    Difference between a real and a fake, 7
    Modern, 6
    Orthodox, 79
    Satanic, 5, 11, 61, 62, 63
    Sephardic, 9
    Talmudic, 84
    Ultra-Orthodox, 9, 79
    Zionist, 51, 57, 59
Jewish, 4, 8, 9, 10, 11, 13, 17, 21, 22, 24, 27, 28, 29, 30, 31, 32, 33, 34, 35, 36, 37, 38, 40, 42, 44, 48, 50, 57, 59, 61, 63, 64, 67, 68, 69, 79, 82, 85, 91, 92, 93, 94, 95, 97, 98

K

L

M

N

U

V

W

Y

Yakub, 46
Yellen, Janet, 64

Z

Zadok, Izahk, 58
Zionism, 32